Murdo Mackenzie

View of the salmon fishery of Scotland

Murdo Mackenzie

View of the salmon fishery of Scotland

ISBN/EAN: 9783743345478

Manufactured in Europe, USA, Canada, Australia, Japa

Cover: Foto ©ninafisch / pixelio.de

Manufactured and distributed by brebook publishing software (www.brebook.com)

Murdo Mackenzie

View of the salmon fishery of Scotland

VIEW

OF THE

SALMON FISHERY OF SCOTLAND

WITH OBSERVATIONS ON THE NATURE, HABITS, AND INSTINCTS OF
THE SALMON; AND ON THE LAW AS AFFECTING
THE RIGHTS OF PARTIES, ETC.

BY THE LATE

MURDO MACKENZIE

ESQ. OF ARDROSS AND DUNDONNELL

Rien n'est beau que le vrai.
BOILEAU.

WITH APPENDIX

WILLIAM BLACKWOOD AND SONS
EDINBURGH AND LONDON
MDCCCLX

CONTENTS.

	PAGE
INTRODUCTION,	vii
PREFACE,	1
SECTION I. PRESENT STATE OF THE SALMON-FISHERY,	5
... II. NATURE, HABITS, AND INSTINCTS OF SALMON,	12
... III. STAKE-NETS,	42
IV. RIGHTS OF PARTIES,	58
... V. SCOTTISH STATUTES,	85
... VI. RIVERS, FRITHS, ETC.,	103
... VII. MR KENNEDY'S COMMITTEE,	113
... VIII. CLOSE-TIME,	135
... IX. TROUTS,	147
APPENDIX,	167

INTRODUCTION.

On the occasion of giving publicity to the following treatise, Mr Mackenzie of Ardross and Dundonnell avails himself of the opportunity to subjoin in an Appendix a discussion on the affinity of the species of salmon with that of grilse—the result of close observation and protracted practical experience—to supply the only omission in his father's production, written thirty years ago, on the nature and habits of salmon; as well as to throw out suggestions on the interesting subject for naturalists to meditate upon, and for praiseworthy experimentalists to clear away the obscurities that surround them.

DUNDONNELL HOUSE, ROSS-SHIRE,
April 1860.

PREFACE.

It is universally admitted, that the history of Salmon and the true nature of the Salmon Fishery—the causes of its decline, and the means of its improvement—are yet but very imperfectly understood. That we have much to learn relative to the natural history of this fish, as well as of all other fishes, whose movements are in an element where they cannot be traced, is most true; and this will probably continue to be the case for a long period of time, unless some friendly Mermaid, or other inhabitant of the deep, shall kindly supply us with information upon points which seem at present utterly beyond human power to ascertain or elucidate. Yet there are many *facts*, with reference to Salmon, which we *do* know, and which may at least enable us to form a pretty correct opinion of the nature of the Fishery. Indeed, all the knowledge relative to the habits of the fish that is useful, or which seems necessary for the benefit of the Fishery, Providence has placed within our reach: it is only those parts of its history which it would merely gratify our curiosity to learn, that are still hidden in darkness; and even these, as well as other operations of Nature with which we are yet unacquainted, may, possibly, like the power of steam, be in time developed—each new discovery exciting fresh wonder, and all showing the immensity of the Power and of the Intelligence by which the whole was created.

It would be ridiculous in one who, from long experience, knows well what we are acquainted with, and what we are not, to attempt to write anything like what may be termed a *history* of the fish in question. Nothing, indeed, can be farther from his mind than any pretension of the kind; but, observing the errors which are afloat on the subject, and the great *injustice* to individuals which those errors have occasioned in the Courts of Law, to whose decisions the decline of the Salmon Fishery in Scotland may perhaps be more ascribed than to anything else, he has deemed it a sort of duty to those whose properties are in jeopardy, or who may have to stand up in defence of their just rights, to put the following observations upon paper, in the hope that others, better qualified to do justice to the subject, will follow his example, from a similar sense of *duty*, and that thus a better system may be ultimately brought about.

It will undoubtedly be deemed a high degree of presumption in one who knows so little of Law, save from the suggestions of common sense, to meddle with it at all. But Law in Scotland, in nine cases in ten, is nothing else than the mere accidental opinion of the Judge, varying with his knowledge of the subject before him; and, in truth, the administration of justice is so intimately connected with the state of the Salmon Fishery—so interwoven with its very existence—that they cannot be separated. The Court of Session holds, in fact, the fate of the fishery in its hands: it may ruin it by declaring the most destructive modes of fishing legal—for the will of the Court is law; or it may prevent the possibility of its improvement by tearing up the rights of the owners of the rivers in which the Salmon are produced; for the idea of improving it elsewhere, as will be shown, is all delusion and nonsense.

We abhor *injustice* in every shape, from the very bottom of our soul. Where it is the consequence of ignorance, negligence, or incapacity, it is an evil of the most malignant description, which strikes equally at the interests of individuals and the security of society.

To the public the improvement of the Fishery must ever be a subject of considerable interest; since the quantity of luxurious food which may be derived from this source, under a proper system, is incalculable. As the population of the country becomes more dense, more land may be brought into culture out of the millions of waste acres in the kingdom; but the number of the Salmon rivers cannot be increased,—*they* must remain FOR EVER stationary. No species of property is, therefore, likely to become of more value to individuals; and there is none more deserving of protection, with reference to the public, though upon none has so little been hitherto bestowed.

Much cannot be expected from a mere salmon-fisher, *qui devient barbouilleur de papier malgré lui*, and whose hand an OAR would suit much better than a pen. All he can pretend to is experience of the fishery. He has killed salmon with stake-nets and with coble-nets, with cruives, spears, and rods,—in the tide-way and out of the tide-way, and has paid deep attention to all their motions, having really a friendship for the whole persecuted race; and if the *facts* he states cannot be controverted, or the inferences that result from them be denied, he cares very little about the style in which they are expressed. If salmon-fishers minded such bagatelles as style, grammar, or othography, neither a late author, the salmon-fishing patriarch of Dochnalurg, nor himself, would venture to put pen to paper. All he asks is to be judged with candour and impartiality, if such things there be; for, to say truth, he has met with very few of these exotics in his journey through life, the corner of the country where his unlucky stars have placed him being of too barren a soil for the generous plants to thrive in. Where his statements do not carry the conviction of truth with them let them be condemned at once without mercy. They are only presented as mere sketches for others to follow up; and the greatest gratification he can receive is, that they will do so, since truth must ultimately prevail. It is like a fishing-cork, which may be kept for a time under water, but will at last get to the surface. *Au reste*, the same points recur so often in different parts, that repetition may be expected without ceasing; repetition, besides, refreshes bad memories ; but, says a French author, *Q'importe la route pourvu qu'on arrive au but ?* and our *but* is, that the TRUE nature of the fishery and the obstructions to its improvement should be better understood.

VIEW, &c.

SECTION I.

PRESENT STATE OF THE SALMON-FISHERY.

"LOOK BEFORE YE LOUP."
Scotch adage.

It is a fact admitting of no dispute, that salmon, which were formerly so plentiful in the rivers both of England and Scotland, have, for a considerable time past, become comparatively scarce. In England, indeed, the fishery has fallen off to an enormous extent; in Scotland it has long been fast declining, though, happily, it has not yet reached the same state of depression as in the sister country. This seems to be in the natural course of things. In all unimproved and partially civilised countries, such as the western coast of North America, the rivers are full of salmon; while, in the rivers on the eastern coast of that continent, where, in former times, the fish were equally abundant, they have now become scarcer, and will, doubtless, continue to diminish in numbers in proportion to the increase of population and the improvement of the arts of life. And the reason of this is plain; for all animals which nature has brought within the reach of man, and fitted to minister either to his comfort or subsistence, must necessarily become less numerous the more they are destroyed; especially when, as in the case of salmon, the rate of multiplication or increase depends, in a great degree, upon causes over which we have no manner of control. When destruction, therefore, is pushed beyond a certain limit scarcity must ensue. It is thus that Nature punishes us for the abuse of the benefits she confers upon us; it is thus that our rapacity comes, in time, to defeat its own objects. No animals are so easily destroyed as salmon, because none are brought, by their habits and instincts, so much within our power, in returning to the rivers; and hence there is a corresponding danger that destruction may be carried further than the generative powers of nature can replace.

Formerly, when the modes of fishing in use were less exterminating than at present, such destruction could not, or at least did not, take place; and, accordingly, salmon were then plentiful both in England and in Scotland. Servants of farmers used to stipulate with their masters that they should not be obliged to eat salmon except on a certain number of days in the week. How different is this from the state of matters at present, when salmon, instead of being a common article of food for the poor, have become a luxury for the rich, and when the supply and the demand frequently vary in an inverse proportion! The cause, however, is abundantly obvious. As the population increased in numbers and in wealth, the destruction of the fish became greater than the powers of nature could replace or restore, and scarcity was the necessary consequence.

In Scotland, previous to the last thirty or forty years, the quantity of salmon caught being greater than an immediate market could be found for, they were salted; but the price of salt-fish was then so low as to offer no inducement to overfishing; so that the rivers kept full of breeding fish, while the aggregate amount sent to market continued nearly the same. It is deserving of notice that, in many rivers, the salmon-fishery used then to be nearly over by the end of May; in some of the late rivers indeed it continued somewhat longer; but the salmon-vats being by this time generally full, the grilses were deemed of so little importance that one-half of them was not destroyed. Yet, at the period referred to, 1000 barrels of salmon were exported from fishings which do not now produce *one-third* of that quantity. But there was then, it will be observed, scarcely any fishing of salmon on the coasts; the whole was confined to the rivers, and carried on by means of what the stake-net fishers are pleased to call the rude fishing apparatus of our rude ancestors; although they have forgotten to add, that it has always been among rude nations, and by means of rude fishing machines, that salmon have been caught in the greatest abundance.

In England, as we have already remarked, the salmon-fishery has declined in proportion as the population and riches of the country have increased. In Scotland, the discovery, by the late Mr George Dempster of Dunichen, of exporting salmon in ice to the London market, has contributed to produce the same effect, by raising the price of the fish, and thus stimulating the salmon-fishers to a greater destruction of the species. From this period, accordingly, may be dated the commencement of the decline of the Scotch fisheries; which, though comparatively trifling at first, has latterly been accelerated in a ratio which threatens, at no distant period, the entire extinction of this important branch of national industry.

The rise of price occasioned by the means which Mr Dempster's discovery had furnished, of sending salmon in a fresh state to the London market, not only rendered the fishers more assiduous and industrious in their fishing operations, but proved a strong inducement to employ new and more destructive modes in capturing the fish. Hence stake-nets were introduced from the Solway into the Tay, and thence into all the other friths in Scotland; and vast quantities of salmon were caught in these engines—quantities which were represented as so much absolute gain to the public, inasmuch as, but for these admirable engines, they could never, it was said, have been caught at all! The stake-nets, accordingly, became quite popular, and were regarded as a great practical discovery. To keep up the delusion, their owners maintained that the supply of fish was perfectly inexhaustible; that the sea literally swarmed with them; that salmon were as numerous as haddocks along the coasts; and that nothing was wanting but effectual means of capturing them, which *their* apparatus alone supplied. And all this the public believed, because the public knew nothing whatever of the matter. But the owners of the rivers, whose properties were thus destroyed, maintained, on the other hand, that the supply of fish, so far from being inexhaustible, was, from the very nature and habits of the salmon, necessarily limited; that, in point of fact, their fisheries had decreased exactly in proportion as the stake-nets were productive; and that, consequently, there was no absolute increase of supply, as the owners of the stake-nets had pretended, nothing, in short, except an increased capture at some points, and a correspondingly diminished capture at others. By all who know anything of the subject, these are now admitted as unquestionable truths, yet nobody believed them. It was universally supposed that the opposition of the river proprietors to the new engines arose, not so much from the alleged interception of the fish, as from the ruin of their monopoly, as it was termed, consequent on the introduction of these machines, and from a selfish desire of keeping up the price of salmon in the market. They were branded as monopolists, who would be content with nothing short of a monopoly price for their .commodity; while the generous and liberal owners of stake-nets were recommended to public favour as men who, having augmented the supply, sought no more than the rate of the market, whatever it might be. *In point of fact, however, the market price of salmon never fell one farthing below its ordinary average level, even while the stake-net manner of fishing was at its height;* and it would have been marvellous if it had, seeing that, in truth, no additional quantity of fish had been sent to market, and the former relation between supply and demand remained undisturbed. But, notwithstanding this decisive fact, the plausible fallacies of the stake-net owners continued to be credited; and no regard whatever was paid to the statements of the " fresh-water proprietors," as they were derisively called, either by the public, or in the courts of law, where the new engines were protected as far as the law would possibly permit.

Some of the judges compared the river heritors to men who would wish to prevent their neighbours raising superior crops of grain, lest their own should, in consequence, fall in price. But there is obviously no analogy whatever between the real case and that which these learned persons supposed, for the purpose, it may be presumed, of illustrating it. Indeed it seems never to have occurred to them, that such a combination as that implied in the supposition is as impracticable as it is absurd. If one farmer raises a superior crop, another may do the same. Each looks to his own interest; his object is to raise as much grain as possible himself, whatever others may do; and he knows that he must take his chance of prices. The idea of combination, in such a case, is utterly ludicrous. In the same way, what haddock or herring fisher ever thought of preventing others from fishing, that the price of his capture might thereby be enhanced? The thing would never enter his imagination except as the subject of a jest, and even in that case would speedily be dismissed as a very stupid one. But if the operations of one set of farmers or haddock-fishers were of such a nature as to interfere materially with those of another, and to diminish, in a great degree, the product of their labours, as well as to neutralise a large portion of the capital invested in their respective employments, a new and very different question would arise, namely, whether such interference was consistent with that equal protection which is due to all kinds of property, and whether one man is entitled to avail himself of the advantages of a peculiar situation to enhance the value of his own property at the expense of his neighbour's, or, which comes to the same thing, to the utter destruction of rights secured to the latter by unchallenged titles, and exercised by him from time immemorial. Now, this is precisely the matter at issue between the stake-net men and the river proprietors. The question is not, whether two men shall fish where there is unlimited abundance, and no possible interference of rights or pretensions; but whether one shall fish in such a manner that the other shall not fish at all, although his title be at least equally good, and the exercise of his right fortified, perhaps, by ten consecutive prescriptions.

Were salmon like sea fishes, the stake-net owners would, in that case, have some reason to complain of the opposition of the river heritors, and of the hardship of not being allowed to kill salmon as they might kill cod, haddocks, or herrings. But as there is not a salmon in the sea but which, from the very law of its nature, *must* come to the rivers, it is obvious that every fish intercepted by a stake-net is taken from some river fishing or other; and that, while the public gain nothing whatever in consequence, the owners of the rivers are deprived of their natural and legal rights by this interception of the fish. In short, the effect of the new system is merely to produce a *transfer* of property from one set of proprietors to another; to enrich the stake-net owners, who have neither right nor title to such a boon, at the expense of the river heritors, whose properties have been secured to them by the strongest muniments of title and prescription.

In the meanwhile, the fishery, as might be expected, continues to decrease, on the whole, more rapidly than ever. If, as has already been observed, the salmon-fisheries, in all countries, decline in proportion as wealth and population increase, from the constant and growing destruction of the species, the addition of so many new modes of destruction, since the invention of stake-nets, must necessarily serve to aggravate the evil: and such, accordingly, is the *fact*. Instead, therefore, of encouraging modes of fishing, which evidently trench deeply on the sources of supply, and must ere long cut them entirely off, the object of the legislature and of the courts of law should be to *restrain* the capture of the fish by every means in their power, consistent with the fair exercise of the rights of property. This they could easily do by restricting the mode of fishing, in all parts, to the movable coble-net. But the courts of law, from mistaken notions relative to the fishery, have hitherto done just the reverse, and have given every encouragement to fixed nets, which they conceive can do little or no injury to the rivers; as if salmon dropt into them from the clouds, or were in the same predicament with haddocks, herrings,[*] or cod.

This conception, or rather misconception, however, has been singularly disproved by the result. The fishery, as already stated, has been progressively declining, and more rapidly, too,

---

[*] Since this was written the notion has been growing, that herring may be over-fished as well as salmon, and this has helped to lead to the prohibition of the trawl, or circle net, by 14 & 15 Vict. Cap. 26.—ED.

than before the introduction of the fixed nets. This is a fact so perfectly notorious that it cannot be disputed or denied. In order to remedy the evil, a new Act of Parliament has been resorted to for the protection of the breeding fish in the rivers, to the destruction of which the stake-net owners of course ascribed the decline of the fishery, which has been greatly accelerated by their own engines. Of this act notice shall be taken hereafter. The destruction of the breeding fish is undoubtedly a great evil, which has prevailed at all times, and formerly, we believe, to a much greater extent than of late years. Where the breeding-fish are killed, however, the effects are immediately visible in the scarcity of young fish. But it is not here that the decline of the fishery is by any means most conspicuous, since the young fish are comparatively plentiful and constitute now, in effect, the staple of the fishery ; a proof that the alleged destruction of the breeders is *not* the principal cause of its decline. It is of grown fish that there is the greatest scarcity, because from the multiplicity of fishings, and modes of destruction, the salmon are not allowed to attain their full size. Indeed there is hardly a full grown salmon now to be seen, at least not one for a score that were formerly caught, which could only happen from over-fishing. If all the lambs and year-old sheep in the country were killed, would not mutton be scarce ? It is the same with salmon. And if they grow from five to eight or ten pounds each in a year, and are almost all destroyed in the early stages of their growth, must not the fishery, from this cause alone, be, on the whole, in a declining state ? The weight or absolute quantity of food thus lost to the public is immense ; and until this evil be remedied, which can only be done by restraining fishing operations in the manner already hinted at, and affording the necessary protection to the rivers, it is idle to expect that the fishery can ever be brought to a proper state of improvement. If the public want to have abundance of salmon, let the salmon-fishers be compelled to return to the rude apparatus of their ancestors, so much ridiculed by our modern stake-net poachers, but in reality the only mode compatible with the preservation of the fishery, and the regular supply of the market. *Hacc hactenus.*

SECTION II.

ON THE NATURE, HABITS, AND INSTINCTS OF SALMON.

"La nature de toute principe des choses est le secret du Créateur. Notre nature —celle de l'univers—celle de la moindre plante—tout est plongé pour nous dans un gouffre de ténèbres."—*Voltaire.*

SALMON, like herrings, are both a gregarious and migratory fish. Hatched in rivers, they perform a migration to the ocean, whence they return periodically to their natal streams; and they form themselves into gregarious collections, or shoals, composed of separate tribes, or families, belonging to the respective rivers, which keep distinct from each other during the period of their migratory abode in the sea.

Some have called the salmon a *sea* fish, merely because it performs a temporary migration from its native river to the ocean. On the same principle, a parrot, born in India, which has passed his life in this country, may be called an English bird. A salmon is a true highlander, born amid the mountains, but who, like other highlanders, goes to forage elsewhere. A salmon, which returns to an early river in December, will not leave it till after it has spawned the December following,—thus remaining near twelve months in the river. Some even go the length of saying that salmon breed in the sea, as if they had ever seen different or contrary instincts exist in the same species of animals; but Mr Hogarth's experiment has proved, what, indeed, required no proof, that the thing is impossible; for, having reared fry in a bottle, the *ova* which he put into salt water perished; and even some of the fry, which had been removed into salt water at an earlier period of their existence than when they naturally proceed to the sea, died. Yet one of the luminaries of the Scottish bar, distinguished for his grave eloquence, declared, that if all the rivers in the kingdom were blocked up, salmon would become more plentiful than ever, as they would then be *forced* to spawn in the sea. This gentleman, who is no naturalist, will make an excellent *judge* in fishing cases.

Even in rivers salmon are never known to deposit their spawn in deep, or in still water, or in lakes, but on fords, where the stream runs rapidly. Sir H. Davy supposed the reason for this to be, that the water is there more saturated with fixed air, but the bottle experiment shows that this is not the case. The true reason may be traced to the spawning operations themselves, in which the exertions of the spawners are greatly assisted by the action of the water in streams; they commence their operations at the lower extremity, shedding the *ova* and milt as they proceed, so that in working upwards, the gravel, thus stirred, is carried down by the strength of the current, and covers the spawn as it is deposited. In still water this would not be the case; nor, unaided by the current, or action of the water, could the fish make the necessary furrows; their instincts, therefore, which in all animals are perfect, point out to them the proper place for their operations. The process of spawning has been so often described, that it is useless to repeat it. A late writer has represented it as resembling that of a hen digging a hole in the earth or sand with her wings, the spawners lying on their sides, making the furrows, or removing the gravel by a quick jerk and curvature of their bodies, principally with the fins and tail. At this period they are always accompanied by a horde of river trouts, who often are very alert in picking up the *ova* as they drop, and the male spawner is every now and then seen chasing them away. Theorists, or closet salmon-fishers, and even stake-net fishers, as Mr Halliday, who, in regard to the true nature of the salmon-fishery, are little better than closet-fishers, tell us that, as there are from 16,000 to 18,000 *ova* in a female salmon, six or eight pair of fish would be sufficient to stock the Tay. What becomes, says Mr Halliday, in the committee, of all these ova? Poor simple soul! let him ask the river trouts, and eels, and water ousels, and other birds that are constantly preying upon them, and upon the fry in their infant state, when no bigger than needles, and to whom his 18,000 *ova* would scarcely make a breakfast. Even when going down to the sea, clouds of seagulls hover over them, darting down every instant and picking them up; and after they have reached the sea, they are no doubt devoured by all other fishes, according to the universal law of the marine regions. But the greatest destruction of all, in the Scotch rivers, of both the *ova* and fry, is by severe and rapid winter floods, which in some instances tear up the spawning beds, so that scarcely a vestige of them is left, covering the adjacent meadows with ova and fry; while in other parts such quantities of sand and gravel are thrown upon them, that the spawn is quite smothered. If Mr Halliday and his stake-net friends happened to be taking their morning walk along the banks of a river on one of these occasions, and saw the meadows strewed with ova and fry, they would no doubt see the necessity of sending for a few *additional* breeders to repair the loss. There is, however, but one practicable cure: namely, to keep the rivers always well supplied with breeding fish, so that, if much of the spawn be destroyed, much will have a chance to escape. It is the only way by which the quantity of salmon can be *increased.*

The salmon which enter the rivers in the early part of the season, in the spring and summer months, which, though all charged with spawn, the stake-net fishers do *not* consider breeding fish, are always the very best and surest breeders, because they are enabled to reach the higher parts of the rivers, where, the quantity of water being less, the spawning-beds are not so liable to be destroyed by winter floods. The fish which do not enter the rivers till towards the conclusion of the season or close-time (and these are often very few in number, as the fish *then* become scarce), which the stake-net fishers and our theorists think quite sufficient, seldom ascend beyond the lower parts of the river, where the spawn is exposed to the whole force of the water, enlarged by the various streams that fall into it, and is often swept away in the manner we have stated. Fish ought, therefore, to be allowed to run up the rivers at all periods of the season; but this cannot be done without a considerable sacrifice on the part of the river proprietors: and is it likely, or natural, or reasonable, to suppose that they will, voluntarily, make this sacrifice, for the benefit of the coast proprietors, who, by intercepting the fish when returning from the sea, would reap the principal advantage resulting from it? This is one of the great evils arising to the salmon-fishery, from the system of the Scotch Court in giving every encouragement in their power to the coast proprietors, at the expense of the river fishings.

The number of salmon in a river, granting that it is sufficiently stocked with breeding fish, depends upon its length, the extent of its spawning grounds, and the number of its tributary streams. In all these particulars the Tay and the Spey stand conspicuous among the Scotch rivers, and they accordingly produce by far the greatest quantity of fish; but if salmon entered rivers only as chance directed, as the stake-net fishers tell us, it is evident that all those advantages, or the number of fish bred in a river, would not be of the least use to its fishery, as the fish would take the first river they met with, and another river, possessing none of those advantages, and in which a single salmon was not bred, if situated more in the *course* of the fish, would kill the greatest quantity. This would be so contrary to experience, and to common sense, that we find the advocates of the chance system themselves, even where their rivers are in such remote situations that no chance fish would apparently reach them, incurring considerable annual expense for the preservation of their breeding fish, which is a tacit acknowledgment of their being conscious of the reverse of what they say.

Salmon spawn in different rivers at different periods of the season. Those which come earliest into a river, and reach the higher parts, generally spawn sooner than those below. In all rivers it seems necessary that the salmon should remain some weeks in the river previous to spawning, and they are generally several days on the spawning-fords before the operations commence. Mr Home Drummond's Act[*] has, therefore, trenched greatly on the spawning season, in the early rivers, as well as

[*] 9 Geo. 4, Cap. 39.—ED.

curtailed the number of breeders, by extending the period of fishing eighteen days beyond the usual time. When on the fords the breeders are easily destroyed. A man may then kill them sometimes with even a walking-stick, in the higher parts of the rivers, and in the streams where there is often scarcely water sufficient to cover the back fins, so much are these fish brought by their instincts, from the depths of the ocean, within our power. The thief who steals a sheep from a common is hanged; but the greater and far more destructive thief, who, without a particle of more right, steals the breeding fish, containing 18,000 *ova* each, and which are then rendered by nature lean, black, slimy, and disgusting, is only fined a mere trifle; yet, whether with reference to the proprietors of the fishery, or to the public, his offence is unquestionably infinitely the greater of the two. Such is the *consistency* of our laws, the wisdom of our Legislators, and the discrimination of our Judges.

After the spawning operations are concluded, the spawners, then denominated kelts, or spent fish, retire to the sea. The kelts generally drop down the river during the winter and early part of the spring, in so exhausted a state, that many of them are found dead on the banks. At this period vermin are found in the gills of the spawners, that is, after spawning, but are never found save in kelts, or spent fish; though the stake-net fishers would wish to have it supposed that they attack all salmon in rivers and force them to return to the sea, which is not the case, for after a salmon has entered a river it never leaves it till it has spawned; nor, as we have just said, are vermin ever found in their gills till then. Whether such vermin be the consequence of their emaciated state after spawning, as in the case of other animals, or to what cause they may be imputed, is one of those secrets of nature to which we have not the key.

Every river, and even every branch or tributary stream of a river in which salmon are produced, *has a variety of the species peculiar to itself, and which return regularly to it from their migration to the sea.* This is an important fact in the history of salmon, not merely with reference to the natural history of the fish itself, but also in a *legal* view, for regulating the rights of parties, as will be hereafter shown ; and we must, therefore, as it seems to be still doubted by many, be permitted to dwell upon it at some length. In one river, for instance, a large breed is found, averaging, perhaps, twenty pounds weight, while in the very next river there is a small breed, averaging scarcely seven pounds. In some rivers the salmon are long and narrow, or lank ; in others broad and short—so broad and so short, that when cut up they are nearly circular. In one river we find all the salmon straight in the back—in another, round or hog-backed. In some rivers their heads are all large and clumsy— in others, small and neat. Even in the spots and scales there is often a visible difference. In short, the distinctions are so numerous that it is needless to detail them. The salmon of some rivers are so strongly marked that a stranger would recognise them at a glance,—while he could only be sensible of the distinctions between those of others by comparing them, when the difference would strike him at once. Now, when salmon of exactly the same shape and description, and no others, are uniformly found in the same river, where can there be room for doubt on the subject? Or how could this be the case if they did not return to breed in it? Will any man say it is possible it could be so, if other or different breeds entered it—that is, if salmon entered rivers by chance, or promiscuously? When, then, people talk of the particular fish of different rivers, under the chance system, they speak nonsense, since, under such a system, all the breeds would be mixed together—so that a river, like the Shannon, which had a large breed one year, might have a small breed the next. The *fact* of the different varieties found in the different rivers, admits of even *legal* proof, if the evidence of the senses can be deemed so. Many doubt it, for no other reason than because they think it wonderful ; but what is there in the works of nature, when closely examined, that is not so? If no two human faces, or voices,—no two flowers,—no two leaves of a tree, are absolutely alike—if the varieties of nature are boundless— where is the great cause of wonder that each salmon-river should possess a variety of the salmon species belonging to itself?

When Nature, then, or rather Nature's great Author, formed all these varieties of the salmon race, and planted one in each river, it was certainly not that they should be all lost by promiscuous intermixture; and he, therefore, engrafted instincts into them, sufficient for perpetuating what he had made. By the gregarious instinct, each variety, or tribe, is made to shoal by itself, unmixed with other varieties, even in the sea; and by another powerful instinct, all are made to return from their migration, with perfect regularity, to their native rivers; by which means the whole varieties of the race have been continued as they were originally formed. And it is the same with herrings, of which each loch has its own variety or distinct breed.*

If salmon entered rivers by chance, it is plain that they would all go into the first river they met with, if all could get into it without choking up its course, and that the rivers in remote situations would have none; or a river might be full of fish one year, and be quite deserted the next—without even a breeder. How different this from the manner in which all now get regularly their share, in consequence of the instinct which brings the fish back to their own rivers. A straggling fish of one river, may, no doubt, sometimes go into another, because the organs of a salmon may be diseased as well as those of another animal; but this seldom occurs. It may also happen sometimes, that when a shoal or tribe of salmon are scattered, either by their natural enemies, or by stake-nets placed on their course, when returning to the rivers, a stray fish belonging to one river may mix with and follow a shoal belonging to another river, as a stray sheep will sometimes mix with a flock of passing sheep; but even if the salmon should accompany the strangers into their own river, he would soon leave it, if not killed, and return to his own. We have heard an instance of such a salmon being taken and marked, and allowed to escape, and retaken in his own river next day at a distance of forty miles.

We know that some salmon-fishers, whose experience has

* There is not, too, a trout loch or stream in Great Britain, or, as Sir H. Davy remarks, in Europe, that has not its own variety of the trout species.

been limited to fishing on the coasts, or at the mouths of great rivers, though they do not absolutely deny that salmon return to their native rivers, do not admit the fact, because they are ignorant of it. These men, finding salmon of different shapes in their nets, suppose it is the fish of different rivers. They do not reflect that there could be no different breeds belonging to different rivers, if salmon entered all rivers by chance : the inconsistency never struck their minds. These fish were, however, the salmon of the different branches of the same river, caught by them, at or near its mouth ; all which would proceed up the common channel, and strike off, each into its own branch, or natal stream, as it reached it. The upper fishers, or the inhabitants in the vicinity, could point out with ease the fish of each branch ; they could sort them as a shepherd would different breeds of sheep ; but the sea fishers, whose sole object is to catch all they can, never give themselves the trouble of investigating such matters. It would be absurd, however, to consider ignorance of a fact as proof of its non-existence, in the face of positive proof to the contrary.

All intelligent salmon-fishers, indeed, who have had the means of knowledge on the subject, fully acknowledge the fact. Even Mr Little, the celebrated stake-net fisher, admits it. He states, in the Committee,—

" I believe every river has a peculiar breed of fish, both as to salmon and grilse. We have three fishing rivers that fall into one bay in Ireland, the Bush, the Bann, and the Foyle ; and we can *easily* distinguish the salmon of the different rivers when we take them. The salmon of the Bush is a long-bodied round fish, nearly as thick at the head as it is at the middle. The salmon that we kill at the Bann is what I call a very neat-made fish, very broad at the shoulder, and the back-fin tapering away towards the tail, and quite a different shaped fish from the Bush fish. In the Foyle we get few salmon but grilses. The Shannon fish are very large, few of them under twenty pounds, and many of them thirty and forty pounds and upwards. The salmon that are bred in the Bush never get larger than nine or ten pounds. A large salmon never will come from a small breed : a Bush salmon would never grow to the size of a Shannon fish, though he were to live to any age."

The Committee ask Mr Wilson of Berwick,—

"Can you inform the Committee whether salmon, bred in a river, and going to the sea, return to the same river, or go to other rivers, as accident may lead them?"—"I am fully of opinion that every river has a peculiar breed of salmon. They all return to the same river where they were bred."

"Have you ever known, during any season, the salmon quit the river Tweed, from any accidental cause, and run to any other river?" —"No, never. I have attended a few weeks in the year at Montrose, where there are two rivers, the North and South Esks, and the species of salmon is quite different in these rivers."

"Do you mean to say that you yourself, from your own knowledge, could distinguish a fish of the North Esk from one of the South Esk?" —"Yes."

"Can you describe the distinction?"—"One is a large, coarse, scaly fish—the other is a small and finer fish."

In a communication from Sir George Mackenzie, of Coul, to the Chairman, he states,—

"But the principal *fact* to be ascertained is, whether salmon, bred in a river, *uniformly and certainly return to it?*—That they do is, I think, *beyond dispute:* not only so, but that each river has its own variety or tribe of fish. I know more than even that: for it is a *fact* that three varieties of salmon, quite distinct from each other, enter the river Conan, and that two of these belong to its two *branches*. I one day happened to be angling below the junction of its lower branch, with a party of strangers on a visit to the late Lord Seaforth at Brahan Castle, when, by a singular chance, I killed three salmon, one of each variety, and I showed them to the gentlemen with me. The variety that belongs to the main river is a handsome fish, being considerably broader, in proportion to its length, than the others; the salmon of the upper branch, the river Rasay, or Black-water, are more round and full, and are reckoned the best (in quality) of the three varieties. That belonging to the lower branch, the river Orin, is a long lank-looking fish, and is little esteemed when compared with the others."

The same facts have likewise been stated by other persons many years ago. A gentleman in the vicinity of the Tay, in an Essay* upon Salmon, says,—

"Each river has evidently distinct fish of its own, which with a

---

* Prize Essays.

wonderful instinct explore their way to their parent stream. From the sea they run to the Tay, from the Tay to the Isla, and through that river for several miles, till they come to the junction of the Ench, where, without exception, every fish ascends, and then leaves the Isla, none going up it further. Those spawned in the Linth are known to take their course up the Rhine; out of that river up the Aur, through the lakes of Zurich, and so into the Linth. In like manner, through various rivers, lakes, and windings, they push up to the very interior parts of North America, on purpose to breed in the natal waters.* There are, however, some instances of animals mistaking their instincts. The flesh-fly has been seen to deposit its eggs in the flower of the fetid stapelia, deceived by the resemblance of its smell to that of carrion. So I have known salmon to run up rivers in which they were not bred—but this seldom occurs. I remember a circumstance of the kind when angling in the Ench. I caught a salmon, whose figure appeared to me very singular. It had a hogged back, something resembling that of a perch. I showed it as a curiosity to a fisherman who was near me, and asked him if he had seen the like before? His reply was, Yes; that is a Tummel fish: it has lost its way and strayed up here."

Another acute observer † of the nature of fishes remarks,—

"Salmon, it is well known, form gregarious associations, into which only those are admitted which belong to the same tribe or family. So much is this the case, that the salmon of one river is never known to run up another, though they might easily mistake their way when the streams are muddy. As an example of this, it may be stated that the rivers Forth, Teath, and Allan, form a junction near Craigforth, and each contains salmon that are easily distinguishable, both in size and shape, from the others; yet the salmon of one of those rivers are never known to enter the others, though the streams are often swelled from excessive rains."

In the same way, another writer,‡ a practical salmon-fisher, who had the fact daily under his eyes, states,—

"That every river, in which salmon are bred, has its own peculiar fish, and that the salmon of one river differ in appearance from those of other rivers, are *facts* known to every person in any degree acquainted with the salmon-fishery. In proof of this it may be mentioned, that the river Berridale in Caithness, of which I am tenant

* Sir Alexander Mackenzie's Travels.   † Survey of Forfarshire.
‡ Prize Essays.

is formed of two rivers, which hold their courses at nearly four miles from each other till within four hundred yards of the sea, where they unite. One of those rivers produces a short thick fish, the other a long and lank one ; when the salmon return from the sea they go each into their own river, as naturally as a horse goes to the stable to which he has been long accustomed, and there is scarcely an instance of a fish entering the river of which he is not a native.

" It is no less remarkable that, when we fish in the *sea*, near the mouths of the conjoined rivers, we find the salmon *in two separate shoals:* and it very seldom happens that a fish, originally of the one river, is found shoaling with those of the other."

The *grand* point, then, that each salmon river possesses a variety of the species peculiar to itself, and that all salmon are forced, by a powerful instinct, implanted in them for the purpose of continuing or perpetuating those varieties, to return from their migration to the ocean, to their natal waters, may, we think, be thus set at rest; and if this is the case, it must be quite obvious that, if there were a thousand stake-nets, or other fishings on the coasts, of either the sea or estuaries, they could add nothing to the general supply, or catch a single salmon, save by *interception* on its progress to its river. The farther we trace the instincts and habits of the fish, the stronger and more invulnerable will this truth appear.

The fry, or smolts, become vivified towards the beginning of March ; and about the middle of April they begin to descend the rivers in their migration to the ocean, always keeping together in close ranks or shoals, even in going down the rivers, on their grand migratory voyage. To what regions of the deep these little beings, led by nature from their parent streams, and the kelts, or spent fish, direct their migratory course, is one of those points in the history of salmon which has, in all ages, puzzled the most experienced salmon-fishers to ascertain ; which we can do nothing more than form random conjectures about, and which is likely to continue in darkness, unless, as we said, some friendly mermaid shall whisper a word of information into the ear of some favoured fisher on the subject. Some persons have supposed that salmon do not go far from the land, but we never could learn that they had any grounds for thinking so, or that a single fact could be adduced in support of their opinion. In general, the fishermen believe that they migrate somewhere to the *north*, as it is from thence they are always observed to come, which is all they know of the matter. The Committee ask Mr Bell of Perth, a salmon-fisher of great experience,—

"Where do you think the salmon come from? where do you think they winter?"—"I believe that is a *mystery*."

"What do you suppose?"—"I believe they come from the *north*."

Dr Fleming is asked by the Committee,—

"Where do you think the fry and spent fish proceed after their descent to the sea?"—"The question is one of extremely difficult solution; but the following circumstances may be mentioned, as throwing some light on the subject. They do not retire to the sea-shore, otherwise the stake-nets would succeed in capturing the kelts at least; and if they frequent the nearer banks on our coasts, I should think it probable that the bait employed by our fishermen to catch the different kinds of white fish, would occasionally tempt a hungry kelt. It is not known that such fishermen do take such kelts, consequently I would be disposed to conclude that the fry and kelts betake themselves to deep water, at a *considerable distance* from the shore—indeed *to parts with which we are wholly unacquainted.*"

In all this we agree entirely with the Doctor. The only question seems to be, to *what* remote regions of the deep they do retire; and in solving this insolvable question, we are thrown, as we have said, wholly on speculation and conjecture. Let us, then, take a look at herrings, between whom and salmon there are so many analogies, to see if it will assist us on the subject.

It is beyond dispute that all the herrings which constitute our herring-fishery are bred on the banks around our coasts, and in the sea-lochs and friths by which the northern parts of the kingdom are indented. In the Cromarty Frith nine cart-loads of herring fry have been taken out of one yair in a tide: in another yair, in the frith of Inverness, at Tarradale, the fry, principally those of herrings, are often sold by the bushel; and in the frith of Dornoch, at Kincardine, the swine have been usually fed with them. The fact, then, that the herrings spawn in the sea-lochs and estuaries is, obviously, beyond all doubt ; and it is equally indisputable that the herring-fry, while in their infant state, perform a migration from their natal waters to distant parts of the ocean, just as their little neighbours the fry of salmon do from the rivers.

Now, it is pretty well known that the fry of herrings migrate to the Polar Sea, from whence they are seen to return annually, their course being distinctly marked by the clouds of sea-birds which hover above them, among whom the solan goose and *arctic* gull, both birds of high latitudes, are conspicuous. Herrings, too, like salmon, are gregarious fishes, forming themselves into divisions, or tribes, or families, composed of the herrings of each bank, or sea-loch, which keep separate from each other, even when collected into one great shoal. Thus Mr Headrick remarks,—

"The general opinion is, that the herrings retire to the Polar sea, or frozen ocean, and from thence move southward, in one immense mass, in June. On the outside of this great shoal whales are often seen, while an immense assemblage of sea-fowl form a belt, or zone, above it farther than the eye can reach, and whose screams are heard, even when too remote themselves to be visible. This great shoal is composed of *subordinate* shoals, or subdivisions, which keep separate by themselves, as an army is composed of battalions."

And Mr Pennant observes,—

"The great rendezvous of the herrings is within the *arctic* circle. There they continue many months, the seas within that space *swarming with insect food* in a degree far greater than in our warmer latitudes. The mighty army begins to put itself in motion in the spring. We distinguish this vast body by that name, for the word herring is derived from the German *Heer*, an army, to express their numbers. They begin to appear off the Shetland Isles in April and May : these are only the forerunners of the grand shoal which comes in June, and their appearance is marked by certain signs, and by the numbers of birds, such as gannets and others, which follow to prey on them : but when the main body approaches, its breadth and its depth is such as to alter the very appearance of the ocean. It is divided into distinct *columns*, and they drive the water before them with a kind of rippling. Sometimes they sink for the space of ten or fifteen minutes, then rise again to the surface, and in bright weather reflect a variety of splendid colours, like a field of the most precious gems, in which, or rather in a much more valuable light, should this stupendous gift of Providence be considered by the inhabitants of the British Isles.

" The first check this army meets in its march southward is from the Shetland Isles, which divide it into two parts; one wing takes the east, the other the western coast of Great Britain, and fill every bay and creek with their numbers: others pass on to Yarmouth. Those which take the west, after offering themselves to the Hebrides, where the great stationary fishery is, proceed towards the north of Ireland, where they meet with a second interruption, and are obliged to make a second division: the one takes to the western side, and is soon lost in the Atlantic; but the other, which passes into the Irish Sea, rejoices and feeds the inhabitants of most of the coasts that border upon it. Were we to consider this partial migration of the herrings in a moral light, we might reflect, with veneration and awe, on the mighty Power which originally impressed in this most useful body of His creatures the instinct that directs and points out their course, that blesses and enriches these islands, which carries that, at certain and invariable times, to quit the vast Polar deeps, and offer themselves to our expecting fleets. It is not from defect of food that they put themselves in motion, for they come to us full fat, and on their return are almost invariably observed to be lean and miserable."

Another later writer [*] of great intelligence states,—

" It appears from various reports that all the herrings which visit the British shores proceed, in the month of June, in one great body, from a high latitude, and from *a great distance*, to the north-west of the Shetland Isles. On one occasion particularly, this immense shoal was discovered by Provost Finlay of Campbeltown, an experienced seaman and herring-fisher. Many leagues to the north-west of Shetland he passed through a shoal of herrings, the extent of which he estimated at *twenty leagues* in length, and four or five in breadth. At this time they seemed all to observe the same course, their heads being directed the same way, which was to the south-east. The weather being fine, the shoal came sometimes to the surface of the water. This great shoal, when it approaches our coast, divides itself into two divisions, one of which takes the west, the other the east coast of the kingdom, *sending detachments into the different*

[*] Dr Walker.

bays and lochs as it passes. It is thought by some that, after the herrings have spawned in our shore, they return to the deep, but not far distant from our coasts, where they remain at the bottom till next season; but they have never been discovered in this situation, and no herrings have ever been known on our shore, except what proceed from the northward of the Shetland Isles, from whence they pay their regular annual visit to the coasts of Scotland."

This is confirmed by a great practical herring fisher*, who remarks,—

"It is the opinion of some that the great shoals of herrings never retire to any considerable distance from the coasts of Scotland: this, however, is a mistaken idea, because, if this were the case, they would be found in the stomachs of large fishes, such as cod and ling, of which great quantities are taken on the coasts, yet none are found in the stomachs of these fishes during the absence of the herrings, whereas, after their return, three or four full-sized herrings are frequently found in the stomach of one of these fishes. There is, therefore, every reason to believe that the herrings proceed, *in the state of fry*, to the Northern Ocean, whence they return periodically when they come to maturity. This is farther proved by the *facts*, that the farther north the earlier the fishery commences, and that when the herring shoals first approach our coast they are accompanied by whales, and by *Arctic* gulls, whose plumage differs from that of other gulls."

From all these facts, then, there seems little reason to doubt that the herrings, which are bred on our coasts, perform, as fry, a migration to the Polar Ocean, from whence they return annually, full grown, with perfect regularity, in one immense mass, formed of separate subdivisions, or tribes; that, on reaching our coast, this immense mass divides into two parts, one of which proceeds towards the Irish Channel, and the other takes its course along the east coast, both throwing detachments into the various lochs and bays as they pass. Those detachments, however, the above writers seem to suppose are thrown into the lochs from the main body by mere chance: they have not traced the operations of nature with sufficient minuteness: they left the most wonderful part of this grand system unexplored: if they had considered that each herring loch has a

---

* Mr John Mackenzie.

distinct variety of the species belonging to itself, as each salmon river has its own breed or variety of salmon, they would have seen that the separate subdivisions, or tribes, of which the great shoal is composed, are the distinct families or tribes belonging to each loch, which detach themselves from the main body, and enter their respective lochs as they reach them, just as the salmon enter their own rivers.

Dr Walker, indeed, states, "It may be questioned whether or not herrings return to the place where they were spawned, as on this point I could obtain no certain information." The only information, however, which it was possible for him to obtain on the subject, was the simple *fact*, that the same distinct variety of the species was uniformly found in the same loch. This fact alone was sufficient; because, as with salmon, it could not *exist*, save by each returning to breed in its own loch, and to no other. The thing would be quite impossible, since, as we have remarked with regard to salmon, all the varieties of the species would be blended together by promiscuous intermixture. Why, it may be asked, did Nature, which has done nothing in vain, or uselessly, or without a purpose, engraft into herrings, as into salmon, the *gregarious* instinct of collecting into tribes, each composed of a distinct variety of the species, and of preserving themselves from intermixture with other tribes? What other purpose could there be for it, save the one we have stated? Mr Headrick, who seems to have bestowed much attention on the fisheries, remarks, "No Highlander was ever more averse to spurious intermixture with other clans than herrings are to associations with other tribes. I have been told of two shoals meeting, which crossed each other with some confusion, but without an individual of the one shoal associating with the other. In fact, a discerning eye, assisted by the sense of taste, can perceive a difference of quality and frequently of size, between the herrings which frequent the different lochs."

This difference is, in fact, acknowledged universally. The fishermen at Loch-duich can distinguish the herrings of that loch from those of Loch Long, though the two lochs are only separated from each other by a narrow point of land; and at

Loch Erebol, and Loch Glendhu-beg, when a herring of a different loch is found, amid a mass of their own, the fishermen say, "Here is a stranger, let us see what loch he belongs to." But we need not go farther than Lochfyne, the quality of whose herrings is known to all. These herrings have uniformly retained their character of superior excellence. Has this been owing to the food? No, for in the great shoal all the herrings feed alike. Is it casual? Is the quality good one year and bad another? No, it is the same every year, as far as memory can trace. This, then, could only happen in consequence of the gregarious instinct which makes them cling to each other and shoal in a separate division, or tribe, in the great mass, and return to breed in their natal loch, without intermixture with inferior tribes; and, assuredly, these instincts were not infused into the herrings of Lochfyne alone, but were engrafted in the whole race. In some lochs the herrings are so large that 800 will fill a barrel; in others it requires 1100, and in some 1500. An experienced herring-fisher has remarked, "These distinct sizes certainly formed one great shoal before they entered the lochs, but must have gone in separate divisions or squadrons from each other, otherwise how is it *possible* that the size of herrings caught in each loch is found nearly equal, that is, without there being a mixture of small among the great, or of great among the small?" The reason is just the one we have stated. There can be no other. Each loch gets its own herrings. The large breeds do not mix with the small, nor the small with the large. If they did, the whole would be one mongrel breed, instead of the distinct and wonderful varieties with regard to quality, as well as to size and shape, which exist, and which have existed from the beginning, and are continued and perpetuated by invariable and perfect instincts.

Sir H. Davy has observed, with reference to the instincts of bees, that "the laws of a perfect, social community, as it were, are adopted by beings that we are sure cannot reason. In the hive-bee, for instance, the instinct of the workers leads them to adopt and obey a queen; and if she is taken from them, or dies, they have the power of raising another from offspring in the cells by an almost miraculous process: they work under her government for a common object, allow males only to exist for the purpose of impregnating females, who preserve the society, and under whose government they send forth swarms, who readily place themselves under the protection of man. In the geometrical construction of their cells, the secretion of wax from their bodies, the collecting of food, and the care of the brood, there is a series of results which it requires a strong reason to follow, and which are the consequences of perfect instincts."

But what can be more wonderful than the instincts of herrings?—the fry, scarcely two inches in length, proceeding from the various lochs and banks around the kingdom, all in one direction, to the Polar Sea—congregating there in one immense mass, in separate and distinct tribes—returning altogether in that mass, regularly, at a stated period of time, yearly;—this immense mass, on reaching our coast, forming itself into two divisions—the one taking the west, the other the east coast; and each tribe so admirably, so systematically *stationed* in so vast a mass, that, when it divides, all the tribes belonging to the lochs and banks on the east coast, should fall, with perfect regularity, into the one division, and the tribes of the west coast into the other: a tribe belonging to the Moray Frith never following the western division to Lochfyne or the Isle of Man, nor the tribes of those parts straying with the eastern division to the Moray Frith or Yarmouth.* Let the immensity of the shoal observed by Provost Finlay, *sixty* miles in length, and from twelve to fifteen in breadth, all in one mass, be only contemplated, and then the marvellous arrangement of the tribes in this mighty shoal will be duly appreciated. When shall all the *arcana*—all the wonders of nature be developed to man? Not till thousands and thousands of years shall have rolled over his head—if ever.

We have heard it said that herrings sometimes desert a loch for years and go elsewhere. We do not believe it, any more than we believe that salmon can forsake their river. It would

* If this were not the case, while the superior herrings of Lochfyne were found there one year, the inferior tribes of the Moray Frith, or Lochroag, might be found there the next.

be contrary to the general law implanted in their nature : Deleterious ingredients, as lime thrown into the water, might probably kill all the salmon in a river, but would not make them abandon it, and go to another river. We cannot conceive that an instinct, engrafted from the creation in a race, can cease its operation, or abandon them for a few years, and afterwards return again into them. It would be an anomaly totally beyond our comprehension. If Nature works by general laws, nothing can overset those laws. The herrings of a particular loch may, by over-destruction, be rendered so *scarce*, that the few that do return may be deemed undeserving of notice ; or they may be liable to accidents we are unacquainted with. Such scarcity, we know, has been complained of at Lochroag. The herrings of that loch are of a particularly large breed, harsh in the flesh, and fibrous, and easily distinguished from those of other lochs ; yet we never could learn that during their scarcity there they were found elsewhere, though they would be recognised at a glance amid the herrings of the other lochs.

If, then, the herrings perform a migration to the Polar Sea, we think it very probable that salmon, which, as we said, have so many analogies in common with them, migrate to the same regions ; for we can see nothing more extraordinary in the fry of salmon, bred in our rivers, doing so, than in the fry of the herrings, produced in the friths and bays into which those rivers discharge themselves. It is evident that the salmon retire to a considerable distance from land ; for, exclusive of the reasons adduced by Dr Fleming, there can be no doubt that if they remained in the seas around our coasts they would sometimes be observed by the crews of the vessels that are constantly navigating those seas, which is not the case ; they would, too, be at all times flocking into the rivers : there would not be that periodical, regular, annual return, of shoal after shoal, as at present ; and, besides, we do not think there would be *food* in our comparatively barren seas for the great quantities of salmon and grilses that are produced in all our rivers. They evidently do not live on haddocks, whitings, or mackarel ; and the few sand-eels that are on our banks would afford very little sustenance to such numbers; but herrings are found frequently in their stomachs, and they all return fat and full fed, which shows that their migration is performed to regions abounding with food. Even the herrings fall off when they come into our seas. Dr Walker observes, " During the residence of the herrings on the coast of Scotland we know of no food they use, no sort of palpable aliment being found in their stomachs, and during all this time they become gradually leaner." These are, therefore, not seas for salmon to get fat in.

But the case is very different in the *arctic* seas. We have been informed by the crews of whale ships that those seas abound with a sort of mucilage, evidently intended by nature as food for fishes. Mr Pennant, as we have seen, remarks, "Those seas *swarm with insect food*, in a degree far greater than in our warmer latitudes;" and Dr Walker states, "In the seas in those parts a *vast profusion* of a singular substance is seen floating on the surface, *to such an extent*, as to make the sea appear *as if covered with oil*, — but has been nowhere observed on the coast of *Scotland.* If this account, given by persons of observation and veracity, is correct, we need no longer be surprised at the retreat of the herrings to those tracts of the Northern Sea, nor at their return from thence in a full fed and fat state." If, then, the salmon migrate thither they must have food in great abundance.

Those seas, indeed, appear as if formed by nature as a grand nursery of fishes, which abound there to an infinitely greater extent than in more southern latitudes. The numbers taken on the coast of Norway, all the way to the North Cape, show this. Von Buch states, that the fishery at the Vaage alone employs 18,000 men and 4000 boats. "The yearly arrival," says he, " of the cods at the spawning-banks takes place with regularity. After spawning they return to the ocean, either in quest of *herrings*, or to unknown regions of the deep ;" and Brooke tells us, that "the fishery at the Loffoden Isles gives employment to 25,000 men and 5000 boats." "The fish," says he, " come invariably from the *north*, and pass on to the southward." The great numbers of seals, too, found in those seas by the whale ships, whose cargoes are often in a great degree made up of them, also shows that fish must abound there ; and these fish were assuredly not formed by Providence for seals alone. The rich mucilage, with which those seas are covered in such profusion, seems peculiarly adapted to afford nutriment to the hordes of herring fry, which repair thither annually, and would do so too to the fry of the salmon, as these, when grown, would feed on the herrings themselves, which supply food for so many fishes, and which are so frequently found in the stomachs of the salmon when they first come upon our coasts that many salmon-fishers consider them as their common food. The wonderful progress of the fry from our shores to those parts is, of course, regulated by their instincts. "Sometimes," says an author already cited, "the herrings swim slowly, at other times they go faster than a boat can row." Perhaps the fry, on leaving our coasts, are directed into under *currents*, which may possibly carry them quickly to their destination.

If we look to what appears to be the principles of the migratory system, certainly not the least curious or the least beautiful in the scheme of the universe, this migration of the salmon and herring tribes to the *arctic* seas will be found in perfect accordance with it. In taking a glance at this singular system, there are some circumstances so obvious that they must strike all. First, all the great migrations of the migratory tribes are invariably made to *distant* parts: next, they are made *annually:* and lastly, they are always made in groups or *masses*. All these circumstances we trace to the migrations of herrings and salmon, in common with the tribes of migratory birds with which we are acquainted, such as the swallow, the lapwing, the woodcock, Teal duck, &c., which must, necessarily, come from a great distance before they reach our shores, which come only once a-year, and whose migratory movements are always made in groups. A gentleman informed us that he once saw a large tree in the churchyard of the parish of Eddertown, in Ross-shire, absolutely covered with swallows, ready to take their migratory flight; and another gentleman stated that he had seen a meadow in Caithness where an immense flock of lapwings were collected, apparently for the same purpose. Any person who has observed a squadron of wild geese in spring, winging their way to the north, must have been struck with the systematic order and regularity with which their migratory flight was conducted. In Macgill's *Travels in Turkey*, it is remarked, respecting the migrations of the stork,—

"These birds pay an *annual* visit to Turkey. They arrive in vast numbers, and always in the night. They arrange their progress very systematically. They send forward their scouts, who always make their appearance a day or two before the *grand army*, and then return to give in their report; after which the whole body advances, and in its passage leaves, during the night, detachments in the different towns and villages on their way.* Early in October they take their departure in the same manner, so that no man can tell from whence they come, or whither they go. A person who, at the season of their departure, was in the habit of coming from the interior, told me, that on his journey the year preceding, he had seen thousands, and hundreds of thousands, of them near the bank of a river, and that they annually assemble there; and when the general sees that his whole army is collected, he, at a given moment, sets it in motion, leaving a detachment to bring up the stragglers."

The migratory *system* seems, therefore, to be regulated by the same general laws in all parts. That salmon and herrings perform their migrations in *masses* is indisputable; that they do so *annually* is equally so; and that they migrate to *distant* parts we think must be evident from the facts we have stated. The very circumstance of their migrations being performed in shoals, or masses, would, alone, afford a strong presumption that they proceed to distant parts, from whence their return could obviously not be so well or so regularly made singly as in masses. Common fishes, which swim about our shores in search of food, do not require to form themselves into gregarious tribes or shoals: to them the gregarious instinct would be worse than useless—it would be an impediment; but to fishes which have to proceed to distant regions, and to return periodically at stated times, it seems absolutely necessary, to enable them to perform their migrations, and, therefore, Nature has implanted this instinct in them. Undoubtedly the great Being, by whom

---

These detachments break off from the main body just as those of salmon and herrings do, each detachment of storks stopping at the place of its nativity, like those of the above fishes. The analogies of the system are obvious.

all was formed, had He pleased, could have supplied food for those fishes in the seas around our coasts: so He could to the migratory tribes of birds in the parts from whence they come; but then, what would become of the migratory system, which, as we have said, forms so curious and so beautiful a link in the order of the creation? Of what use, too, would those inhospitable regions, the Polar seas, be, abounding in fish doomed to remain there as mere food for seals? To send ships to such a distance, to fish for small fishes amid mountains of ice, would be out of the question. While, therefore, other seas facilitate the intercourse between distant nations, and thus render the various productions of the earth common to all, the Polar Sea has its use, as a great nursery or magazine of fishes, which, by the migratory system, are brought regularly within the reach of man, the means of supplying whose wants forms so prominent a feature in the works of creation.

Let us follow up this system a little further. We have already remarked that the same habits and instincts are uniformly found to pervade the *same* species of animals throughout the whole of the animal creation. A dog, or a cat, or a sparrow, in Spain or in Russia, or a crow, which is found in so many parts of the globe, differs in no respect, in its habits and instincts in those countries, from the same animal in Great Britain; and as a thrush builds its nest in the Hebrides, so exactly does another thrush in Cornwall. This uniformity of instinct in the same species of animals, in all parts, appears, therefore, to be a general law of nature; and we will venture to say, that however they may differ in size, shape, or quality (as is the case in our own rivers), there is no difference whatever, in point of habits and instincts, between a salmon in Kamschatka and one in the Tweed—every individual of the species being influenced by the same instincts, and subject to the same laws. If, then, all the salmon, and all the herrings belonging to Great Britain are forced, by the law of their nature, to perform a migration to the Polar Sea, the salmon and herrings of the Baltic,* of North America, and Kams-

---

* In Sweden the general opinion is, that all their herrings come from the Polar Sea.—*Cox's Travels.*

chatka, must do so too: All, having the same instincts, and acting under the same laws common to the race, must take the same course—must, necessarily, perform the same migration to those icy regions, which, let it be observed, are equally *centrical* to the whole of them, the whole being produced within the same northern latitudes. What a magnificent scene, then, does this migration of all these tribes of birds and fishes exhibit, performing their grand annual evolutions to distant parts, through the trackless regions of the air and of the deep, with the regularity of clock-work, in obedience to laws eternal and immutable!

The progress of the salmon shoals from the north cannot be traced, like those of herrings, by the birds by which they are accompanied;—yet there are circumstances, even in their course, which tend to confirm the hypothesis we have been stating. When the shoals *first* approach our coasts, they often swim so near the surface, probably to get hold of the fresh water from the land, which floats uppermost, and leads them to the shore, that the ripple they make in the water is seen at a considerable distance. A fisherman of Orkney has informed us that he has frequently observed them always coming from the *north,* some taking the west side of those islands, as if proceeding to the coast of Caithness and the Moray Frith, while others keep the sea-side, as if steering their course for the southern rivers. When one of these shoals approaches the rivers Bighouse or Thurso on the north coast, the fishers at those rivers are always ready, with nets of 200 fathoms in length, to row round them, by which means they sometimes take the fish of various tribes; but it often happens that, when the shoal gets within a certain distance of the land, the headmost fish makes a leap out of the water, which is a signal to the shoal to stand off and alter their course, which the whole immediately do, leaving only the tribes belonging to the rivers in those parts behind. After this the shoal continues its course along the coast, within a short distance of the land, till it meets with another river in its way, when those belonging to it enter, just as the herring tribes separate from the main body, and enter their respective lochs as they reach them, while the rest pass on. Sometimes, however, the salmon remain a little while in the tide-way of the river, where many of them are caught by the river fishers; and sometimes the shoal is broken and dispersed by the stake-nets placed on their course. When they reach their respective rivers, the objects of their *destination*, they never leave them, as we said before, till they have spawned.*

Such appears to us to be the progress of the salmon and herring tribes, led in their infant state, as fry, by nature, or instinct, to their northern nursery, where they grow large and full fed, and return at stated periods, in shoals, like fleets of ships, to their respective destinations, pursuing the same undeviating course, the same *track*, year after year, which their predecessors did 4000 years ago, and which succeeding shoals will continue to follow in all future time, unless the race be destroyed by the blind rapacity of man.

After the salmon get into the rivers, the exertions which they make to push their way up, and to overcome every obstruction in their way, form a singular trait in their history. The stake-net owners tell us they are constantly running down from the rivers again to the sea—an assertion which carries absurdity upon the very face of it. If all the salmon are under the influence of the *same* instincts, which they necessarily must be, it is contrary to common sense to suppose that, while some of them ascend the rivers with ardour, others, after having entered the rivers, return to the sea, before they have effected the purpose for which they came there. The assertion is directly in the teeth of every principle of the migratory system, and rests, besides, upon no proof whatever. We have seen a salmon, in the early part of the season, attempting to push his way up a shallow part of a river, and tried to beat him back with a stick; but after receiving repeated blows on the back, instead of turning down, he pushed his way on, and

---

* Mr Stephen states, in the Committee, "Our cruives on the river Don are so constructed that salmon of ten pounds weight can at all times go up, but none can descend, past the cruives. We fish generally in the pool above the cruives; and if the unspawned salmon returned again down the river, we would undoubtedly catch them there, which is never the case. They are never seen to descend the river, except as kelts, after having spawned."

effected his purpose. A writer on the subject* has truly observed,—

"The exertions which salmon are known to make to overcome obstructions in their passage up rivers are truly surprising. To those who are admirers of the wonderful works of the Author of Nature, no sight can be more gratifying than to observe salmon ascending torrents, and throwing themselves up rocks of such a height as no other fish would attempt. A singular instance of this is to be seen in North America, at the great Bellows Falls, where the fishermen hang arm-chairs, secured by a counterpoise, and catch the salmon as they spring. In the early part of my life, I have, with pleasure not to be described, stood for hours together viewing the salmon when in floods, facing the passage of a waterfall called the Keth, in the river Ench, a tributary stream of the Tay. This rock is about *fourteen* feet high when the water is low, but in floods not so much. At this time the strength of man could not resist the current, while they, with considerable facility, make over it. They sometimes fail in their first essays, but, undismayed, and with an unremitting ardour, they renew the attempt, till they prevail in clearing it."

After they reach the rivers, salmon, as before remarked, like herrings, after they come upon our coasts, seem to require very little food: for the few worms that are washed down from the adjacent grounds, and the flies which flutter on the water, are next to nothing. In the sea they feed well,-whole herrings, as we have said, being often found in their stomachs: if they required anything like the same quantity of food in the fresh water, Nature must have filled the rivers with worms, or other insects, to such a degree as to become a nuisance and pollute the water: but instead of this, the streams are pure, and the stomachs of the fish are so constituted as to extract the necessary sustenance almost wholly out of the water itself. Accordingly, nothing is almost ever found in the stomach of a salmon killed in a river. That salmon rise to a fly, is true ; but let any man examine the fly, and see how little food there is in it, or let him watch the river, and see how seldom salmon rise to or catch at flies. In a pool containing a score of salmon he will not, perhaps, see one rise to a natural fly in four-and-twenty

* Prize Essays.

hours. This instinct of rising to flies seems therefore to have been infused into salmon by a beneficent Providence, if not as a source of pleasure to man, at least as affording him the means of capturing the fish, just as sporting dogs have been given him to enable him to capture game. Angling has been called a cruel amusement; yet many philosophers have been anglers. Doctor Paley was a great angler, and so was Sir H. Davy. All animals are made to die, and having no foreknowledge of death, it signifies very little whether they are killed one way or another. A salmon which was hooked in the eye and escaped, leaving his eye on the hook, rose a few hours afterwards, with the other eye to the fly, and was killed.

Salmon rivers are usually classed as early rivers, and late rivers; and it seems to have puzzled Mr Kennedy and his Committee exceedingly, to ascertain what occasioned a difference between them. In some early rivers the new fish of the season begin to come on in November and December, and continue to do so till April, when the fishery falls off; while, in the late rivers, it is only then it commences. In the former the fish begin to get foul, and heavy with spawn in August; in the latter they continue clean till the middle or end of October; so that, taking the whole together, it is quite clear that, under a proper system, *there might be a constant supply of clean salmon at market during the whole year*, the late rivers ceasing to produce their fish just when the early rivers begin to yield those of the new or ensuing crop; and yet the wise men of our legislature have put the whole upon the same footing, and have directed all the rivers to open and close at the same time.

Some of the *savans* of the north, who think they can account for all the operations of nature, state in the Committee, the reason why salmon enter some rivers at an earlier period than others, to be, that their water, flowing from large lakes, is more pure; yet it is when rivers are in flood, that is, in their most impure state, that salmon are keenest to enter them. Besides, none enter those early rivers save their *own* fish, the purity of the water, it seems, having no attraction for the fish of other rivers. Those gentlemen might have considered, that a fish which enters a river early, must have *left his migratory abode* at an earlier period than the fish of late rivers—and must, therefore, according to their doctrine, have had a foreknowledge of the *quality* of the water that would please him, and where it was to be found. The truth is, that some rivers are so constituted by nature as to produce early fish, while other rivers produce late fish, just as some rivers produce large fish and others small fish; and the instincts of the fish are regulated accordingly—the salmon of each river leaving its migratory abode, and proceeding to the river to which it belongs, at the period the instincts implanted in it for that purpose begin to operate, the principle of perfection, visible in all the works of nature, being traceable to the minutest parts of the whole system. Some rivers produce both early and late fish; because some of their tributary streams possess an early, and some a late, breed of fish—all of which must pass up the main or common channel.

The Rev. Dr Fleming is asked in the Committee,—

" How do you *account* for salmon entering rivers early, when they don't spawn till late in the season?" *—" It is a question of extremely difficult solution. Salmon seem to require a residence of a few months in rivers previous to spawning; but as they are known to enter rivers, four, five, or six months before spawning, it seems to me *extremely difficult* to account for such apparently premature migration, unless we take into account that migration of salmon into rivers is a natural instinct of the species, and that, in certain circumstances, this instinct may *prematurely* exercise its function."

Science is, undoubtedly, a fine thing; it is a pity it should be sometimes so nearly allied, by any of its professors, to nonsense. The answer of the Doctor, we conceive, to be a very singular one. We do not pretend to understand the migration of an animal into its *native* element; and, to use the Doctor's own words, we find it extremely difficult to believe, that knowing, as he unquestionably does, how perfect the instincts of all animals are, and how rarely deviations from those instincts

---

* The Committee might have just as well asked the Doctor how he *accounts* for woodcocks visiting this country; and he would no doubt have given an equally scientific answer.

occur, he can really suppose, that at least half, if not three-fourths, of all the fish of the early rivers, are year after year, with *systematic regularity*, led into those rivers by the *premature* exercise of their instinctive functions. The winter months are, in truth, as much the regular fishing season of the early rivers as the summer months are of the late rivers; and yet the Doctor, who seems utterly ignorant of the distinction between early and late rivers, tell us that all this fishing is entirely owing to a *premature* operation of the instincts of the fish! Here we have science, in opposition to nature, in perfection. The Doctor forgets he told us that the fish spawn in December and January, so that if they require only, as he says, a few months of previous residence in the fresh water, and that those which enter the rivers *four*, five, or six months before spawning, must do so from a premature exercise of their instincts; the *whole* of the summer fish must also be in the same unfortunate predicament—that is, the fishery altogether.

The worthy and Reverend Doctor might, we think, have found, if not so scientific, at least a more *orthodox* reason, in the bounty of Providence, who has formed so many animals evidently for the use of man. He has made the rivers to produce a fish, of the richest quality, in such abundance that the rivers themselves could not supply food for one-thousandth part of them; He therefore engrafted into them the wonderful instinct of migration, by which they are led to distant regions of the ocean, where they grow large and fat, and from whence they are made to return again to the rivers—thus bringing them within the power of man, as an article of subsistence, as well as for the reproduction of the species. If the latter were the *sole* object of their return, it would be undoubtedly answered by their coming all at once in August or September, previous to spawning, and no early rivers would be necessary; but instead of this, from their first appearance in the early rivers in November, till they cease coming in the late rivers in October, every stream-tide brings with it a fresh supply, in some river or other, in constant succession, of clean fish during the whole year. The intention of Providence cannot therefore be mistaken; the whole history of the origin and migration of the fish shows it. But in making this fine present to man, Providence has assuredly given it to an *ingrate*, who, instead of gratefully protecting and nursing the animal, brought so completely by its instincts within his power, for his own use, pursues it in all parts, even almost to a system of extermination, for which he is justly punished by the decrease of the species. When we look to herrings, the same intentions of Providence are visible. Forced by their instincts to migrate to the Polar regions, they are made to return to our coasts, and are thus brought within our power; for no man will doubt that He could have made them breed equally well in the icy seas of the north, had such been His will.

Here we must stop. We have spun the subject out into too great length already for *a Sketch*. There are other particulars relative to the fish in question, which we may possibly take another opportunity to state; unless, as we hope, some other better qualified person shall take up the subject, and render any farther statements on our part unnecessary. In the mean time, we think it must be abundantly obvious to all that the rivers are the true source of the salmon-fishery; and that there, and there *only*, can it be improved. Everything, therefore, which tends to diminish the *interest* of the owners of the rivers in the fishery must necessarily operate as a preventive to its improvement, and prove as detrimental to the public as to the proprietors.

SECTION III.

STAKE-NETS.

"In truth I heard it, Provost; and was glad to hear that the scoundrels had so much pluck as to right themselves against a fashion which would make the upper heritors a sort of clocking hens to hatch the fish that the folks below were to catch and eat."—*Redgauntlet.*

AFTER the salmon have left their migratory abode in the ocean, on their return to the rivers, they proceed, as we have stated, in successive shoals along the coast, at a short distance from the land. It is, therefore, obviously a matter of considerable importance to the fishery, that the *course* of the fish should be kept as clear, and as free from obstructions, as possible.* Formerly, at the periods when the fishery was in its most flourishing state, this was the case, for there was then scarcely even a coble-net fishing to be seen beyond the mouths of the rivers, or if there happened to be one, it seldom extended more than a few yards from the shore; accordingly, the shoals arrived unbroken at the rivers. In this view the ancient Scottish statutes, by which all fixed engines are prohibited within reach of the *tide*, which necessarily embraced the whole seacoast of the kingdom, and consequently the course of the salmon returning to the rivers, as will be afterwards shown, were of essential service to the fishery. Some years ago, however, a new mode of fishing, or species of fishing-apparatus, called Stake-nets, has been introduced into the estuaries, and from thence extended to the sea-coast, by which the salutary enactments of the statutes have been defeated, and from which the most pernicious consequences have resulted, and must farther

* The method of fishing proposed by Mr Russel (in *Edinburgh Review*, vol. xciii. p. 365, and *Quarterly Review*, vol. ci. p. 168), is that, when practicable, river-fishing should be carried on by *one* fixed engine, that would take every fish when in operation, and could be managed to let them pass at will.

result, to the fishery. This fishing-apparatus is formed of a long range of stakes carried out from the shore sometimes a mile into the water, that is, to the low-water mark, with nets and traps affixed to them; the whole forming a barrier of the most formidable description in the course of the fish, and which, it must be evident to all, must not only break and scatter the shoals as they come on, and thus most materially hurt the fishery, as regards the public, but which may be so multiplied on the coasts, as to ruin the river fisheries entirely.*

If we only consider the progress of the salmon shoals along the coast, the effects of such machinery, placed in their way, may be easily conceived. We have already remarked that, in coasting their way, in search of the rivers, they generally keep at a short distance from the land. When a shoal meets with a stake-net, some of the fish are caught in the traps, or cruives, or what is called its chambers, others start off; in short, the shoal is broken and dispersed. The scattered fish, however, always guided by their instincts, gather in again to the land, singly, or in groups, and continue their course with the tide, until they meet with another similar engine, when the same capture and dispersion is repeated. It sometimes happens that, as stake-nets are, as we said, always placed on ground left dry at ebb-tide, the shoals may pass on the outside of some of them at low water; but this is but a partial intermission, for as the tide rises, and the fish are enabled to approach the land, they fall into other engines farther on, so that at length only a few scattered fish reach the rivers singly, instead of whole shoals as formerly. It is, therefore, not easy to conceive a

* Bag-nets are, if possible, still more destructive. Both are constructed upon the same principle, the only difference between them being that the one is fixed by stakes, and the other by anchors, and floated by corks. Stake-nets are always placed on sands, or ground left dry by the receding of the tide; but bag-nets may be set in the *alveus* or deep water, and their arms or leaders be extended an indefinite length, so as in fact to embrace a whole frith. So many bag-nets have been placed in the sea, near the mouth of the river Don, at Aberdeen, that nearly three-fourths of the salmon are, it is said, now intercepted before they can reach the river—by which the river heritors are utterly deprived of their properties. If the object of Law is protection of property, it is not so felt at Aberdeen. But, in Scotland, Law is one thing, and Justice another. They may sometimes meet, but in general Law, or what is *called* Law, kicks Justice out of the field.

more complete destruction of property than is thus occasioned to the river heritors.

In the Courts of Law, where the nature of the salmon-fishery is so imperfectly understood, it is supposed that, unless a stake-net be planted in an estuary, or in the vicinity of a river, it can do but little injury to the river fishery; but any man gifted with common sense must see that the injury must be the same, whether the engine be set in an estuary, or on the coast of the sea, if it be placed in the *course* of the fish; just as the injury to the owner of a mill is the same, whether the mill-water be intercepted, or taken away, at the distance of ten yards or ten miles from the mill. It has been said, that stake-nets increase the supply of fish at market; but if they act, and can only act, by *interception* of the fish proceeding to the rivers, how can they increase the supply, since the increase in one part must, necessarily, be met with a corresponding diminution in another? So sure are the instincts of salmon, that none *can* be taken on the coasts which, if not so taken, would not reach the rivers. It is, indeed, upon the very strength of this instinct that the stake-net system is founded, since, but for it, such timid animals would all fly back at the sight of such formidable machinery; yet they often attempt to *force* their way through the arms, or leaders, where they are found suspended without entering the traps at all, so strong is the impulse which leads them to the river.

The whole of the fish thus returning, that is, the whole of the fish which come on the coast, whether intercepted in the stake-nets, or allowed to reach the rivers, it will be observed, are charged with *spawn*. Every one of them, therefore, if not killed, would become a spawning fish; and as the spawn can only be deposited in the rivers, it is obvious that all of them, from this fact alone, *must* necessarily, from the law of their nature, be on their progress to the rivers. In the early part of the season the roe is small in all salmon, and it increases in size as the season advances, until the period of spawning. The stake-net owners say, that the salmon caught by them would not go to the rivers;—in other words, that when a shoal of salmon, in its progress to its river, comes in contact with one of their engines, the shoal is composed, not of fish all impressed with the same instincts, but of fish with different and even opposite instincts,—some with instincts impelling them on to the rivers, and others with contrary instincts which would drive them back to the sea (though in this view it is difficult to conceive what brought them there), and that it was only the latter which were caught in their engines, the former continuing their course to the river;—but in order to support this insupportable absurdity, they ought to be prepared to show that the fish so caught by them were not, like the others, charged with *spawn*, or at least give some other reason of common sense for the assertion. The Committee ask Mr Bell,—

" Have the fish that are caught in STAKE-NETS roe or milt in them?"—" Every fish has roe or milt in it."

Johnstone, the stake-net fisher,—
" The fish are ALL, more or less, full of spawn."

Stephen,—
" In the early part of the year the roe in ALL salmon is small, and it increases in size as the season advances."

And yet, in the face of all this, Dr Fleming, the naturalist, and the friend of the stake-net fishers, stated in the Committee that, of the 30,000 salmon taken in the stake-nets in the estuary of the Tay, every one of which was charged with spawn, none would have gone to the river! Having admitted that during their migration they retired to *remote* parts of the ocean, the reverend gentleman ought to have stated what he conceived to have been the *object* which brought them back, if it was not to proceed to the rivers; and on what grounds he asserted that they would *not* go to the river—if it was in his power to do so.

The stake-net owners allege, as *proof* that their engines do not kill breeding fish, or, in other words, that they only kill the barren fish that are mixed with the breeding fish in the shoals, which we have stated as a great absurdity, the whole being charged with spawn—that towards the conclusion of the season they take scarcely any fish, the breeders then keeping the channel, or deep water. Thus Mr Halliday tells the Committee,—

"The stake-nets begin to fall off materially as the season goes on. The fish do not visit them half so much when the *spawning* season approaches, as they do during the summer months. Towards the end of August the stake-net fishing falls off very materially. In September we catch almost nothing. The fish then keep the channel or deep water."

Now, we have already stated, that there is not a salmon taken, either at a stake-net or river fishing, at any period of the season, but would, if not taken, become a spawning fish—the whole, without a single exception, being charged with roe or milt, increasing in size as the season advances. If one compares the roe of a salmon caught in a stake-net on the first of May, with the roe of another salmon taken on the same day, at a river fishing, they will be found to be *exactly* in the same state: if the experiment be repeated on the first of August or September, the same result will appear. There is no difference whatever between them—both, therefore, as we have said, if not killed, would become breeders or spawning fish; but the stake-net fishers, in order to impose upon ignorant persons, endeavour to make it be supposed that only the last fish which come in would be breeders. The reason why their sea-engines kill few or no fish in September is obvious; nearly the whole of the shoals of the season have by that time passed on, and there are no more fish to kill. Mr Halliday could not, indeed, have stated a fact more confirmatory of our statements in regard to the migratory movements of the fish, or that could tend more completely to contradict his own doctrine; for if salmon were always swimming about the shores, like haddocks, and if the sea, as he says, abounds with them, they would be caught in his sea stake-nets in September, as well as in June or July; but they are only caught, or rather intercepted in them at the periods when the shoals of the season are passing on to the rivers. After the shoals have passed, and there are no more fish to intercept, he, poor innocent, thinks they then keep a different *track*.

Of the grand migratory movements of the salmon tribes, from the ocean, along the coast, to the rivers, shoal succeeding shoal, the stake-net fishers seem to have no conception. They admit their gregarious associations, like those of herrings, and yet seem to think that the gregarious instinct was implanted into them for no purpose, while swimming about the shores like haddocks. They tell us that they are driven into the rivers by sea-lice, without adverting that the assertion is utterly incompatible with the gregarious instinct,—for if the lice can force individuals to leave the shoal, they must, of course, overcome the gregarious instinct which keeps them together. This idea of lice impelling salmon to proceed to the rivers is a very absurd one. When a shoal of salmon leaves its migratory abode in the ocean, in obedience to instinct, or the law of its nature, to proceed to its river, it must accomplish its *destination*, whether any of the fish of which it is composed have sea-lice or not; yet, according to the stake-net doctrine, after the shoal had reached the estuary, only those fish which were infected with lice would go to the river, and the rest, after amusing themselves on the banks for a little while, would return back to the sea, unless intercepted by them,—though every fish they take is just as much infested with these lice as those which are taken at the rivers. The whole of their arguments, indeed, form one mass of inconsistency and absurdity. They will, perhaps, next tell us, that the migratory birds are sent to us by *vermin*, and not in consequence of instincts connected with the migratory system,—and that when a migratory flight reaches our coast, the whole tribe is not actuated by the same instinct, but like salmon, have different and even opposite instincts; some of them having the instinct of remaining, while others, on the contrary, after they reach our shores, set off again immediately to whence they came, just according as they were, more or less, troubled with lice.

Suppose we were to put the following questions to Mr Halliday :—You say that the salmon are driven into the rivers by lice.—Who told the salmon that fresh water was a cure? How did you discover that salmon knew, or have found out this secret? Did a seal tell you so? Why did not the salmon taken in your stake-nets, all of which had lice upon them, go also to the rivers? You say you intercepted them returning to the sea,—were they carrying back their lice to the sea with them, instead of going to the rivers? Perhaps these salmon were not made acquainted with the cure. Have not cods and skate similar lice? Why do *they* not also go to the rivers for a cure? Are not almost *all* salmon infested with these insects while in the sea? Why do they not, then, rise all at once and go into the first river they meet with, to rid themselves of them? Why, under such annoyance, do not salmon seek relief in the nearest fresh water, but, with exemplary patience, pass river after river till they reach their *native* stream? Is it only their natal water that can kill the lice? How do you think the salmon found *this* out? We believe it would not be easy to Mr Halliday to answer these questions. To account for the great operations of nature, or the migrations of animals, by lice, is undoubtedly a rare idea : it is altogether *piquant;*—this *lousy* argument is, therefore, said to have had great weight in the Parliament House, by proving that the salmon are driven, without ceasing, from the sea to the rivers, and from the rivers back to the sea, like shuttlecocks.

In truth, to speak seriously, there is only one *fact*, amid all the nonsense, and all the mass of absurdities, resorted to by the stake-net fishers in support of their pretensions, and for the purpose of enabling them to transfer to themselves, by means of their new machinery, the whole property of the river heritors, and to ruin the river fisheries, by breaking the shoals, and intercepting the fish on their return to the rivers, which merits refutation—namely, that salmon are sometimes caught in the *ebb* cruives of their engines. This fact, however, is easily accounted for; when one once gets hold of the true system, any little discrepancies which seem inconsistent with it only require to be investigated to be blown away. In their progress along the coast to the rivers, the salmon always proceed with the flood-tide, which carries them on to, and ends at, the rivers,* and rest, during the ebb-tide, in eddies, and in easy water ; hence great numbers are always caught in the flood-traps of the stake-nets placed in their course, while comparatively but few are got in the ebb-traps. In proceeding forward, at a short

* "Salmon," says the stake-net fisher, Johnstone, in the Committee, "in the sea, never go against the tide."

distance, as we said, from the land, such as happen to be near the shore after the ebb-tide sets in, when they find the water becoming shallow from the receding of the tide, are led by their instincts to drop down with the tide into deeper water, until the return of the flood-tide enables them to continue their course, and in thus dropping down, some fall within the range, and are caught in the ebb-traps of the engines in question; but it is in the summer season, in dry weather, that by far the greatest number are so caught. At that period, when the rivers are so low that they cannot enter them, their instincts lead them to swim backward and forward with the tide, in the vicinity of the rivers, until a flood enables them to enter them. "It is well known," says Dr Fleming, "that when floods occur in a river, the salmon, *ready to ascend*, speedily enter upon their upward migration. In truth, the fact is so notorious, that anything like personal testimony on the subject is unnecessary. There are many things connected with a river in a flooded state suitable to the ascent of the fish. As the water in the river increases in quantity, the shallow parts of the river become deeper and better fitted to enable the salmon to pass over them, and at the same time the artificial obstacles in the form of milldams, and the natural ones in the form of falls, are all diminished in force, so that the flooded state of the river is the one best fitted for the fish to ascend, *and the instincts of the fish seem to be regulated* accordingly." Again, Mr Hogarth states, "If the rivers were in a state to receive them, I believe the salmon would *all* go up the rivers as they come upon the coast; but the water, during the summer months, is frequently so low, that great numbers of the fish* keep floating backwards and forwards with the tide, until a land-flood takes place, when a great burst of them go up at once."

Is it any wonder, then that, when the fish are thus floating backwards and forwards, waiting for water to carry them into the rivers, they should be taken in both the ebb and flood cruives or traps of the numerous engines with which the coasts are lined? Accordingly, Mr Halliday, the greatest of all great

---

* Particularly the heavy fish.

stake-net fishers, whose authority will not be disputed, states in the Committee,—

" In the whole course of my practice in fishing, I have always found, *in dry weather in summer*, a greater quantity of fish taken in the nets placed for the purpose of catching them with the EBB-tide, than in wet weather. At the time the stake-nets at the Newby fisheries are most successful, the river Annan is at that time so *very small*, that the fish in general would not enter it, and most of them are taken in the stake-nets with the *ebb*-tide."

Here, then, we have the fact fully accounted for, out of the mouth of this stake-net fisher himself. If the fish intended, as he supposed, to return to the sea, they would not keep floating backwards and forwards near the shore, within the range of his machinery; they would go out at once into deep water like the kelts. There is not, therefore, a single fact or circumstance stated by these men, that will be found, on investigation, to be contrary to the principles of the migratory system, or to the instincts and habits of salmon, as we have represented them; or which can, in the smallest degree, confirm their own hypothesis—an hypothesis formed of a whole string of absurdities, every one of which is at variance with the other.

The destruction of these flowing and ebbing fish towards the end of summer, by stake-nets, we consider an evil of great magnitude with reference to the fishery, and one of the causes of its decline. In the early months the fish are keen in entering the rivers. If they were equally so at the conclusion of the season, as they always become, as we said before, scarce towards close-time, there would be a danger that there would be a scarcity of breeders, to guard against which nature seems to have intended those flowing and ebbing fish as a *corps de reserve* for that purpose—as many of them would not enter the rivers till they were unfit to be taken; but all these are now destroyed by the stake-nets, by which means the rivers are denuded of the necessary quantity of breeding fish—and so has fared the fishery. This was not the case formerly, when no other fishing implements were in use than the "rude apparatus" of our forefathers—and accordingly salmon were then, it is admitted by all, in great abundance.

The stake-net owners further tell us, that their engines save many salmon from being destroyed by grampuses and seals. We believe they have the contrary effect. That salmon become the food of many fishes of prey, during their migratory abode in the ocean, is very probable; but, after they come upon our coasts, they keep so near the shore that they are generally out of the way, at least of the grampuses, except when the shoals are dispersed by stake-nets, and the fish forced out into deep water, where of course they may be picked up by them. Seals again watch the stake-nets. The seal is an acute and daring animal—a compound of the tiger and of the fox, and knows well where to find his way. A salmon will often escape from a seal, in a fair chase, but when hemmed in by a stake-net, he has no chance of escape. Mr Johnstone, the stake-net fisher, states in the Committee,—for these men have often stated in favour of their engines circumstances which, in fact, have an effect directly the reverse,—

" I have seen seven or eight seals, *ranged in a line*, before a stake-net; *and when they discovered a salmon they were immediately in pursuit.* They break the nets, kill a number, and let away all the rest."

And his brother fisher, Halliday, says,—

" I have seen the seals frequently come and break into the nets, taking what fish they could, and set all the rest away. I have seen one seal, *which frequented a stake-net* at Budden, take either ten or twelve salmon and grilses in the course of two tides; and I have known one seal take six or eight fish in the course of two hours and a half. Indeed, I have often been heard to say, that I thought they would *take the fishing from us altogether.*"

Poor gentleman! The seals appeared to have used him just as he used the owners of the rivers, though they seem to have been the honester depredators of the two. The worthies divided the fish, and left it to the owners of the rivers to hatch more for them to catch. Seals, however, will have their food, *coute qui coute*. That stake-nets aid them greatly in doing so is obvious: the best way, then, is to kill themselves. Such is the way game is preserved from vermin.

Some suppose that the fish taken in stake-nets is of a better *quality* than what is caught at the rivers. They might be better than what used to be formerly taken in the *higher* parts of rivers, after they had remained long in them; but they cannot possibly be better than what is caught in the *tide-way* of the rivers, where nine-tenths of the fish are now taken. We would defy the most fastidious palate to discover a difference between them, or to distinguish the one from the other on the table. Mr Little, who was a great stake-net fisher, states on this point, in the Committee,—

" I do not consider that there is any difference between a salmon taken in the sea, or in a river, provided he is taken soon after he enters the fresh water. If he is taken in the course of a week after he enters the river I do not consider him any worse; but few salmon are allowed to remain a week in the river during the fishing season."

Mr Hogarth,—
" As to a salmon that has been in the river not above a week, I don't suppose that it would be *possible* to know any difference between him and one taken in the sea."

Mr Wilson,—
" There is no difference whatever."*

If we take the fishing altogether, the balance, even in point of quality, is greatly against the stake-net mode of fishing; because the farther the fish advance towards spawning the worse they get in quality, and it is then that nearly the whole are killed in stake-nets, which take few but during the summer months. Thus, the Committee ask Johnstone,—

" Generally speaking, during what period of the year would stake-nets pay the expense?"—" I should think from April till September."

" In what months of the year are the greatest number of fish usually caught?"—" Generally in the months of June and July, but sometimes there are more salmon in May—but generally in June and July. Sometimes in August there are more."

These are, therefore, all very late fish—far advanced in spawn.

* Salmon are always better for being a few days in their native water. It increases, like crimping, the firmness of the fish—insomuch that while a salmon caught in the morning in the sea is soft enough to be boiled and pickled the same evening, one caught in the fresh water retains its firmness, and would break in the kettle if boiled before next morning. The fish-curers or boilers, who are great epicures, always, accordingly, prefer for their own palates fish that have been some days in fresh water.

Now, in the river fisheries, a great part of the salmon are taken during the winter and spring months, when the fish are of much superior quality to the summer salmon, being farther from the spawning time, and the roe and milt being then smaller. Thus, Mr Houy states to the Committee,—

" Salmon are in the *finest* condition in the *early* part of the season, and are valued in proportion to the smallness of the roe and milt they contain, and are less so every day as the season advances."

Lord Clive,—

" The best fish that are taken in the Severn are commonly in the winter months—in November, December, and January ; those which are taken in the *summer* months are very inferior fish, and people are always ill-disposed to purchase them."

Dr Fleming,—

" The fish fall off in value and become lean, in proportion as the milt and roe increase in size."

Mr Little,—

" The nearer salmon come to be in a state for spawning the worse they are in condition—that is, from the month of May they are gradually growing worse till the spawning time."

And yet it is after May, as above seen, that the greatest part of the fish are taken by stake-nets. This, we think, ought to satisfy those who are of opinion that it is by those engines the whole fishery should be carried on, or who would restrict it to the months when the fish are of least value and in the worst condition ; yet Mr Home Drummond, in his late act, has extended the fishing season from the 26th August to the 15th September, in order to saturate honest folks with inferior fish ; while the winter fish of the early rivers—the very finest of the season—must not be taken, and are thus utterly lost to the community, at least those of the rivers in Scotland, though it is not so in England or Ireland.

There is, therefore, not a single tenable argument or fact that can be adduced in favour of the stake-net system—a system which acts, and can only act, by spoliation of the river fisheries ; thus, in truth, reducing the whole arguments and case to be a mere *transfer* of property, as has been already stated. The stake-net owners have made a great clamour about the *addi-*

tional quantity of fish produced by their engines in the Tay, which they state at 30,000 annually, without any injury, they say, to the river fishings; for, even Dr Fleming states in the Committee,—

" I have no reason to think that, during the operation of the stake-net mode of fishing in the estuary, there ever was a decided diminution in the produce of the river fishery."

This, however, was perfectly impossible, from the nature and instincts of the fish. Besides, so great an increase of supply from the Tay alone, in addition to the increased supply from all the other stake-nets in the kingdom, must have reduced the price of salmon at market most considerably; and yet the Doctor in almost the next sentence tells us,—

" It does not appear that the price of salmon fell in consequence of the additional supply from the stake-nets of the Tay."

It did not fall, because there was in fact no additional supply. The supply from the river fisheries, notwithstanding the Doctor's assertion, diminishing in the same proportion in which that from the stake-nets increased. From the accounts produced by Mr Buist, in the Committee, the correctness of which cannot be disputed, as they were extracted, not from his own books, but from the books of the Dundee Shipping Company, by whose vessels the fish from all the fisheries were sent to London, it appears that, during the last three years, when the stake-nets were in operation in the estuary, viz. 1810, 1811, and 1812, the average annual export from the river fishings was only 1665 boxes of fish; while, according to the statements of the stake-net fishers themselves, their exports amounted to 4000 boxes—making together 5665 boxes yearly. Now, during the first three years after the stake-nets were removed, the average annual amount of the river fisheries was 4552 boxes; and during the next three years, after the river had somewhat recovered from the effects of the stake-net system, it amounted to 5930 boxes, being, during these three years, 265 boxes a-year more than was produced by *both* fisheries while the stake-nets were in operation. If we look to individual fishings they will be found to confirm the statement. Lord Gray's fishings, which, during the stake-net system, produced, in two years, only 8534 salmon and grilses, produced in the same time after the stake-nets were removed 46,332. The rent of this fishing, accordingly, which at the former period had fallen to £1205, immediately rose to £4000, and the rent of the whole river fisheries rose from £5101 to £12,005. All this corresponds but indifferently with the statement of the reverend gentleman, that, during the stake-net system, no decided diminution took place in the produce of the river fisheries: This moral teacher ought to have been more sure of his facts before he threw the weight of his evidence into the stake-net scales (however convenient these engines may have been in the vicinity of the Manse) for the purpose of affecting the rights of any set of men: If, as he says, "there were many other situations in the estuary most suitable for the erection of these engines, which were unoccupied," we conclude that, had the whole been occupied, the river fisheries would have been annihilated altogether.

In the other estuaries the effects of the stake-net system were nearly the same as in the Tay. From the accounts produced by Mr John Steavenson, in the Committee, it appears that, previous to the introduction of stake-nets into the Cromarty Frith, his fishing in the river Connon produced in one year 7656 salmon; while, after the Frith was covered with these engines, the same fishing produced, in another year, only 633 salmon; the stake-net having, during the latter year, according to the accounts of Mr James Taylor, intercepted no less than 6500 fish. Both gentlemen being stake-net witnesses, their accounts cannot be doubted.

In the river Ness, again, it is stated in the Committee by Mr Alexander Fraser, that the rent of the river fisheries, sixteen years ago, was £1055, 11s. and that it is now only £124. This witness, who is a stake-net fisher, and a very honest man, is asked by the Committee,—

"Is it consistent with your knowledge that the river fishery has diminished *in proportion as the stake-nets have increased?*"— "IT HAS."

In the same way the Committee ask Mr Wilson of Berwick, who is tenant of the fishing of the river Beauly, which falls into the Inverness estuary,—

"In point of *fact*, to your knowledge, has the fishery of the river Beauly increased or decreased?"—"DECREASED MOST CONSIDERABLY."

"To what causes do you ascribe the decrease?"—"To the stake-nets and yairs in the Frith. The stake-nets destroy the fishery in the river very much. Since 1816 it has been a losing concern."

"Are there any other causes to which, in addition to stake-nets, you attribute it?"—"None that I have heard of."

All these facts are in direct contradiction to the statements of Dr Fleming, and, added to the documents produced by Mr Buist, prove beyond dispute, if, after what has been said relative to the habits and instincts of the fish, any proof were necessary, that the stake-net system has added nothing to the public supply of salmon. To the public the system *must* be injurious, because it is so to the fishery in general;—first, by the dispersion of the salmon shoals on the coasts, which is an evil of the very greatest magnitude;—next, by the excess of fishing which it has occasioned;—and, lastly, by destroying the interest which the proprietors of the rivers have, or ought to have, in the improvement of the fishery, and making them, as the great author has expressed it, mere "clocking hens to hatch fish for others to catch,"—every one of which reasons tend directly to the *decline* of the fishery. On the score of the over-fishing system, the Committee ask Mr Hogarth,—

"Do you conceive that, by any improvement or extension of the mode of fishing now in use, an increased quantity of salmon could be permanently supplied?"—"I do not; on the contrary, I think the fishings are much too assiduously fished at present, and have been for many years. It is owing to too close fishing that the *size* of the salmon has decreased as well as the *number*. We seldom now see a fish above two years old."

"Do you suppose this is owing to the fishery being over-fished?" —"Yes, certainly."

On this point, a gentleman who wrote many years ago[*] on the subject of the salmon-fishery, remarks,—

"The fishing of salmon may certainly be carried on with so much *accuracy* as gradually and greatly to diminish their number; and it is believed that this has already become the case in many of the fisheries in Scotland. The first settlers in the province of New

[*] Prize Essays, 1803.

Brunswick, not many years ago, found the rivers crowded with fish to a surprising degree, but they have pursued the fishery with such industry that for some time the numbers have been very considerably diminished. There is no doubt that the same has also taken place in this country, and that, by unremitting industry in fishing, the number of salmon may and *must* be so *reduced* as to hurt materially the interest of the proprietors and of the *public*."

Another writer says,—

"It cannot be doubted that the species are fast *decreasing—for the genius and industry of man are ever on the stretch to find out new modes for their destruction.*"

The present state of the fishery confirms what these writers wrote near thirty years ago; yet such is the way in which justice is now administered in Scotland—and such the absence of directing principles, that though stake-nets have been declared ILLEGAL in the Frith of Tay, by a judgment of the Court of Appeal,—and though it must be evident, on the plainest principles of common sense, that what is illegal in one frith cannot be legal in another,—it has hitherto been out of the power of the owners of the rivers which discharge themselves into the Inverness and Cromarty Friths to obtain from the Court protection to their properties against the stake-nets in those friths; and the system of spoliation still continues there to as great an extent as ever. Had the Court acted upon competent knowledge of the subject, the judgment in the Tay case would have been the signal for clearing all the estuaries in the kingdom at once of those destructive engines. By dint of petty specialities, by raising up abstract and insoluble questions totally irrelevant to the real subject-matter of the question, by entangling it in the meshes of an endless multiplicity of unnecessary or frivolous details, and, worst of all, by a total ignorance of the true principles upon which the question ought to be adjudicated, the administrators of the law have unwittingly rendered it an instrument for *not* discovering the truth, but, at the same time, all powerful in entailing ruin upon individuals engaged in a hopeless struggle to protect their rights from invasion and their property from plunder.

SECTION IV.

RIGHTS OF PARTIES.

"Quel est donc cette sauve-garde des lois qui laisse la fortune d'un citoyon à la merci de quiconque veut l'attaquer dans les formes juridiques?"
L'Hermite de la Guiane.

WE shall now take a glance at the *rights* of the proprietors of lands situated on the coasts to salmon-fishings, which they conceive entitle them to intercept the salmon in their progress to the rivers by every means in their power, and give them an EQUAL title to the fishery as the owners of the rivers themselves.

The rights of the owners of the rivers to the salmon of those rivers are founded upon the universally acknowledged principle, that a right to property carries a right to its produce—the very ground upon which the proprietors of lands on the coasts claim a right to the corn and sheep produced upon their estates. Salmon are not like animals which are *feræ naturæ*, and belong to no particular property. Each river, as has been shown, possesses its own variety of the species, which BELONGS to itself exclusively, and which is forced by instinct to return to it, and to no other river. The natural right of the owner of such river to its salmon, therefore, is just the same as the right of the owner of a bee-hive to its bees, or of a dove-cot to its pigeons. They constitute, in fact, as Erskine says, his ESTATE. If there were no fishings except in the rivers, each proprietor of a river would get his own salmon, the produce of his own property, and none else, for none else would enter it. The proprietors of the rivers would thus have every encouragement, like the owners of land-estates, to improve their properties, by incessant care, in keeping the rivers always well stocked with breeders, watching the spawning-fords and fry,—lessening the number of their enemies, and taking every other means that would increase the number of fish, for their own benefit and the benefit of the public. Under the present system, as there can be but little motive or inducement to improve, so none of these results can take place; for what owner of a farm would be at expense and trouble for its improvement, if the crops were to be carried off by others? The loss which the public sustain from the present system must, therefore, be obvious.

But upon what principle does the proprietor of a land-estate situated on the coast of the sea, at perhaps twenty or thirty miles' distance from a salmon river, claim a right to its salmon? How can he *connect* himself with them? They do not even trespass on his lands, like bees or pigeons, so as to afford so much as a *pretext* upon which to engraft a claim to them. If they migrate to the ocean, the ocean does not belong to him. The rights of his lands end at the water-edge. He has not a particle of right one inch beyond that more than any other individual of the community, or to the salmon passing in the adjacent water, any more than he has to the birds which are flying in the air over his head. To talk, therefore, of his natural right, *ex adverso* (as lawyers say) of his *lands*, to the salmon belonging to the rivers, passing by in an element to which his lands can pretend no right, is a perfect absurdity. He might as well claim, *ex adverso* of his lands, a right to the ships which are sailing past them. If the owners of the lands have any right at all, it must be a *legal* right, opposed to the *natural* right of the owners of the rivers.

Let us then examine this pretended legal right. We believe it to be, *au fond*, very little better than the other. We are told by lawyers, that the first great principle of the feudal law is, that the whole lands, rivers, and salmon-fishings in the kingdom belong originally to the sovereign, from whom all rights to such must emanate, and who may dispose of them either together or separately as he may think fit. When the sovereign makes a grant of a land estate, the grant conveys a right to the lands and all that is upon them; but it carries no right to salmon-fishings, which, being a species of property entirely *distinct* from land, requires a special grant. The lands may be granted to one person, and the salmon-fishing adjacent to the lands to another. There can, therefore, be no right of salmon-fishing, in a legal view, any more than in a natural view, *ex adverso* of lands, which is mere legal jargon devoid of sense, until a right to such be conjoined to the lands by royal grant.

The next great principle of our law, lawyers tell us, is, that after the sovereign has made a grant of property, it is no longer in the power, or, as they express it, it is *ultra vires* of the sovereign to *injure* it, or to authorise others to do so, in any manner of way. Without this there would be no security to property. No man could call his estate his own. The Crown might be constantly curtailing it, or be granting servitudes over it. It would be utterly valueless and unsaleable.

For example, after the Crown has made a grant of an estate, and it has become private property, it would be *ultra vires* of the Crown to grant even the servitude of a road over any part of it in favour of an adjacent proprietor; or if there was a mill on the estate, the Crown could not authorise such adjacent proprietor to obstruct or intercept, even upon *his own* property, the stream of water proceeding to it, to the *loss* or injury of its owner. No court of law would sanction such an act. It would be deemed quite illegal and of no effect.

Upon the same principle, after the Crown has made a grant of a salmon-river, or, what is nearly the same, the salmon-fishings of a river, it can be no more in the *legal* power of the Crown to authorise conterminous proprietors of lands or others' to intercept the salmon proceeding to the river, than to intercept the water on its progress to the mill. The principle is exactly the same in both cases. We defy any casuist of the Parliament House to make a distinction between them. It is, therefore, clear that all the grants of salmon-fishings to coast proprietors, which, as we have shown, can only act by interception of the fish on their way to the rivers, to the manifest loss and injury of the owners of the river fisheries, *being all made in direct violation of a great and acknowledged principle of the law*, are all necessarily, radically, and fundamentally

ILLEGAL. Such, then, are the boasted rights of the coast proprietors.

When the Crown granted away the river fisheries, all the salmon-fishing property of the Crown was, in fact, exhausted. It had no more to grant, except by taking away what it had already granted—by depriving its grantees, the owners of the rivers, of a part of what had already become their *vested rights*. To say that the Crown had other salmon-fishing property on the coasts to grant, as if salmon were fixed to the lands like oysters, is a perfect absurdity. The salmon merely pass along the coast in their progress to the rivers; and all the Crown could do, if it had the legal power to do so, would be to authorise the proprietors of the lands to *intercept* them in passing, which would be, in fact, a SERVITUDE upon the rivers; but it could not be called a property, though it might be attached to property. Thus, for example, were the Crown to make a grant of a rookery, the rooks, after foraging all day, might, when returning in the evening to the rookery, be killed and intercepted at various parts on their way. Now, suppose the Crown were to grant a right to the owners of those parts or stations where the rooks were so killed or intercepted to do so, which, after having granted the rookery, and it had become the property of another, we conceive it would be not only *ultra vires*, but an act of swindling in the Crown to do; still these stations could not be called *rookeries*, but merely *servitudes* upon the rookery, which might be so multiplied as to extinguish the rookery altogether, and thus deprive the owner of his whole property. And it is thus, exactly, that the Crown has been using the owners of the rivers, by *illegal* grants to the proprietors of lands situated on the coasts, to intercept the salmon in their return to them, and which the Scotch Court are doing all in their power to favour and support, even by means of *illegal* engines, and to the utter destruction of the river fisheries.

That the river fisheries were granted long before coast fishings were thought of is quite obvious. Salmon, when congregated within the narrow limits of a river, were easily caught even in the rudest ages; but it required a considerably advanced state of civilisation before means were invented of taking them in the sea, and accordingly till lately scarcely any have been so taken. Men navigated rivers before they attempted to cross the ocean; and they caught salmon in the streams ages before they ever dreamt that they could be taken in the sea. It is remarked, in one of the stake-net pamphlets, "The modes of fishing formerly in use were efficient in rivers; but from their nature it is obvious they were not applicable to the open sea, or to bays and estuaries. Accordingly there has been very little fishing until of *late* years except in the rivers; *so little*, in truth, that the salmon is vulgarly regarded as a *river* fish."

A clamour has been raised, as we before observed, by the coast heritors, against the owners of the rivers, as possessing a *monopoly* of the fishery. This is much about as just as if a clamour were raised against the proprietors of coal mines as possessing a monopoly of coals, or against the owners of landed property as possessing a monopoly of corn. All possess the produce of their respective properties, and it is the interest of all to render those properties as productive as possible. In this respect, the interest of all owners of property, the salmon-rivers included, and of the public, must always be the same. To call the possession of property, of any description, which is publicly bought and sold at market, and which may be purchased by any, a *monopoly*, is assuredly a great absurdity. We believe what the coast heritors mean is, that a portion of the property of the river heritors should be taken from them, by some agrarian measure, or by the use of machinery, which would have the effect of such a measure, and transferred to themselves. To this we suppose the river heritors would have no objection, if, on the same principle, a share of the lands of the coast heritors were given to them, since it is very certain that the coast heritors possess a much greater monopoly of land than the river heritors do of salmon-fishings. But the coast heritors are not content with the peaceful possession of their monopoly of land, but must covet the fishing properties of their neighbours, as if there were any natural connection between their lands and salmon in a different element—or as if salmon-fishings were not considered as distinct a property from land in law, as they are by nature, until conjoined to land by a Crown grant.

To the public this contention between these proprietors can be of no importance, in any other view than as it affects the market supply of salmon, and we have already shown that that supply, which was at its height, at a period when the fishery was almost entirely limited to the rivers, has been declining in proportion as the coast heritors have interfered with it, and more rapidly since the introduction of new modes of fishing than before. The fishery is scourged into barrenness, and our courts of law seem to suppose the best remedy is to scourge it more, by allowing all species of machinery on the coasts. In the same way, when a land farm is run out by overcropping, the best way to render it fertile would be to crop it still more! To recover the rivers, the owners of the fishery ought, voluntarily, to allow many fish to escape ; but can this sacrifice be expected of the owners of the rivers for the benefit of the coast heritors ? What farmer, as we said before, would be at the expense of liming his land, if others were to carry away the crop? Monoply, truly! If the coast heritors had not a monopoly of the produce of their lands, we believe they would put themselves to very little trouble or expense to raise crops. Honest Rob Roy used to ease their predecessors of a few of their spare stots and heifers, and they wish to do the same friendly office to the owners of the rivers.

One great cause, we may say the principal cause, of the errors committed by the courts of law, in all cases relative to the salmon-fishery, is, as we before remarked, their considering salmon as common sea fishes, like haddocks, swimming about at random, and visiting rivers, as chance may direct, instead of attending to the peculiar instincts by which they are distinguished from other fishes. We trace the effects of this grand error to all their acts, and even to their construction of the law, which cannot be correct when founded on an erroneous principle, or an erroneous view of a subject.

We shall begin, for example, with the rights of the Crown. Lawyers tell us that salmon are *inter regalia*, and belong all to the Crown. That they did so originally is admitted ; but we conceive the Crown has long ago denuded itself of all its right to them, and that, as we said before, after having granted away the rivers, it had no longer any right to the fish of those rivers. This will be best explained by analogous cases of other animals, with which persons in general are better acquainted. Some animals are, by their nature and instincts, capable of being rendered *property*, others are not. Suppose, then, the whole of these animals belonged to the Crown, the Crown in giving away the one would give a right of property, while it could only give a right to take or " *catch*" the other. Thus, for instance, the Crown could only give a right to catch haddocks, for haddocks do not admit, by their nature, of being rendered the property of any. In the same way, take larks, or thrushes, or other common birds, which are attached to no particular part, and have no particular instincts, the Crown might give a right to one man to shoot them in one part, and to another man to shoot them in another part; the one right would not interfere with the other, since none could claim a right of property in such animals. But there are other animals of a quite different description, which, as we have said, do admit of becoming property; thus, pigeons, for instance. If the Crown granted a dove-cot with its pigeons, no man would say, that the Crown granted only a right to kill the pigeons, for that would be an absurdity; the Crown, in making the grant, conveyed the pigeons in *property*, and they, from thenceforth, belonged to their owner, just as much as they formerly belonged to the Crown. And it is exactly the same with salmon rivers, since the salmon are not like haddocks, or common fishes, swimming about at random, but *belong* to the rivers, just as much as pigeons belong to their cots. If only stray or chance pigeons came to the cot, its owner would, then, indeed, have only a right to take such as might chance to come there. He would have no right of *property* in any pigeons: but the pigeons are linked by their instincts to their cot, as bees are to their hives; they *belong* to the cot, and upon this rests the right of property of the owner of the cot to them; yet the instincts by which pigeons are linked to their cots, and bees to their hives, are not half so strong, or half so sure, as the grander and more powerful instinct which conducts the salmon through the extensive regions of the ocean, by the invincible law of his nature, to his native river. What the pigeons are among birds, and bees among insects, salmon are among fishes: they are all property. If the pigeons *belong* to their cots, and bees to their hives, salmon may be said to belong still more emphatically to their rivers; for a pigeon will sometimes leave his own cot and go to another, but a salmon never forsakes his river for another stream. To assimilate salmon, therefore, to haddocks, or other vague fishes, is still worse than to class pigeons, with their peculiar instincts, with larks, or other common birds; nor can the right of property in the salmon be denied more than in the pigeons, both resting on the same instincts, and on the same principles.

Suppose, then, as we said, all the pigeons, and all the bees, and, we may add, all the rabbits in the kingdom, all of which admit, by their nature and instincts, of becoming private property, as salmon among fishes, from similar instincts, do, were, like salmon, *inter regalia*, and belonged to the Crown originally, would it not be a great absurdity to say that, after the Crown had made grants of all the dove-cots and their pigeons, of all the bee-hives with their bees, and of all the rabbit-warrens with their rabbits, as the Crown has done of all the lands and salmon-rivers in the kingdom, to individuals, and that those pigeons, bees, and rabbits, had become the *property* of such individuals, that, nevertheless, they *still* belong to the Crown, because they did so *originally*, before they were granted away? If there were other salmon besides those belonging to the rivers, the Crown would still have a right to them; but there is not one which does not belong to one river or other, nor, therefore, any which, after having given away the rivers, can still belong to the Crown. The Crown is in exactly the same predicament with any other proprietor, who, after having *sold* or disposed of a subject, has no longer any more right of any kind to it, than if it had never belonged to him. The Crown, as we said, in granting a right to haddocks, or larks, could only give a right to *take* them in particular parts; but in granting the dove-cots, including their pigeons, the bee-hives with their bees, the salmon-rivers with their fisheries, the rabbit-warrens with their rabbits, the Crown bestowed all these in *property*, and all the right of the Crown to the whole, or any individual part, of such property, from that moment ceased. In short, the right to any subject must depend on the *nature* of the subject.

That a salmon-river with its salmon is as much a property as a dove-cot with its pigeons, or a rabbit-warren with its rabbits, or even a sheep-farm with its sheep, we think is indisputable. The salmon are bred in the river as the sheep are on the farm, and the instincts by which the one are attached to its parent stream, are at least as strong as those which bind the other. The temporary migratory absence of the salmon can make no difference, for the *certainty* of their return renders the right of property in them as secure as to sheep which may be sent to winter elsewhere. We have, however, heard lawyers doubt that salmon-fisheries could be called property. If a salmon-river is not a property, what is it? Is it a servitude? If it is a servitude, on what property is it a servitude? We know of no other distinction except property, and servitudes upon property—so that if it is not the one, it *must* be, necessarily, the other. But the salmon are, as we said, bred in the rivers, and no animals can be bred on a servitude. A salmon-river is, therefore, a property, or it is nothing. On the other hand, a coast-fishing, or a right to intercept the *passing* fish, which, when they reach the rivers, remain there, can from its very nature be only a servitude—though it may be *attached* to property or land. It is to all intents and purposes a servitude upon the rivers, a servitude which the Crown had no more a right, as we have said, to inflict upon the rivers, than it had to impose servitudes upon lands, or than it would have to authorise the interception of the pigeons returning to their cots. If the right were admitted, it might, as we said before, be so extended in all parts along the coasts, as to occasion the utter extinction of the river fisheries—which, alone, ought to show its illegality, as being absolutely incompatible with every principle of protection to property. If salmon were like haddocks, there could be no servitude on the river properties, because the owners of the rivers could claim no right of property in chance fish which did not belong to the rivers; but we can see no good reason why our judges should view the rights of the proprietors of the rivers in the same light as if salmon *were* like haddocks, any more than they would view the rights of property of the owners of dove-cots, as if the pigeons which belonged to them were like larks or thrushes; or why they should suppose the Crown had a right to impose servitudes on the one more than on the other; or argue about animals as if they were different from what they really are—of salmon as if they were like haddocks, or of pigeons as if they were like larks; in short, why they should prefer a wrong principle to the right one,—the unnatural to the natural—the principle of error to that of truth and common sense.

It is then, as we said, clear that, after the Crown granted away the salmon-rivers, the rights of the Crown were *exhausted*, and that the Crown had no more right in salmon, and no more salmon to give, without taking away what it had already given, and had become the vested rights of the grantees, any more than the Crown, after having given away all the dove-cots in the kingdom, with their pigeons, could have more pigeons to give away, except by taking away those it had already given; or than a man, who had sold or given away *all* his sheep-farms with their sheep, could still have a right to those sheep, or to dispose of them to others, after he had parted with his right to them. In a recent question in the Court of Appeal, the judge put the case, whether, if the Crown had only granted ten furlongs or ten yards of the fishings of a river, the Crown would be thereby precluded from granting the rest of the river? We do not think this is exactly in point to the right of the Crown to grant *servitudes* to the coast heritors to intercept the salmon proceeding to the rivers. How the river fishings were originally granted, whether in detached parts, or as a whole, which was afterwards sold in detached parts by the original grantees, cannot at this distance of time be traced; but the FACT that the *whole* of the fisheries in all the salmon-rivers in Scotland have, under the existing grants, been *possessed* for ages, is beyond all dispute; so that the case put by his Lordship becomes a mere speculative one, which can have no existence in fact. We shall put the same case to his Lordship in another shape:

suppose the whole fishings of a river, the Spey, for instance, for which the Duke of Gordon receives £11,000 a-year of rent,—had been granted to his Grace's predecessors for great public services, which we suppose was the fact, and had been possessed by his family for time immemorial,—and that the Crown should say, There are ten furlongs, or ten yards of land, near the mouth of the river, to which (fishing being distinct from lands) no right of fishing has been attached; we will grant a right of fishing to the owner of these ten furlongs, or ten yards, which will enable him to intercept the *whole* of the fish as they enter the river, and thus deprive the Duke of his property; would his Lordship, notwithstanding the length of possession, sustain the measure, and deprive his Grace of his property? Would he deem it compatible with either law or justice to do so? This very case, thus put, *we maintain to be*, ALONE, *sufficient to refute the* jus tertii *doctrine of Lord* ———,* *and to show that that doctrine, instead of being* LAW, *is founded directly, and pointedly, though not intentionally by his Lordship, on the principle of* ROBBERY *and spoliation, and must, therefore, be as incompatible with* SOUND *law, as it is in the teeth of* JUSTICE *and of common sense.*

And this brings us back to the great principle of protection, which we can never lose sight of, That after a subject, *be it what it may*, has become the vested right of an individual, it is *ultra vires* of the Crown to *injure* it; and, therefore, as we said before, just as much so to injure a salmon-fishing estate as a land estate. The principle is quite clear, and nothing can overset a clear principle, without which there would be no security to property. People may quibble and sophisticate,

---

* Corehouse ought, we believe, to fill this blank. The judge in the Court of Appeal alluded to is Lord Brougham, who advised the judgment of the House of Lords in M'Kenzie (the author) *v.* Houston, August 13, 1831 (reported in 5 Wilson and Shaw, 422), and whose able opinion is well worthy of perusal, though it fails to meet the logic of the text; because it ignores the fact of the certain ascent of the salmon to the river, if not intercepted by engines like Houston's. The technical ground on which M'Kenzie lost his cause was, that he had averred no right of property in the fishing *at the spot* where Houston fished; the strength of the argument for him lay in the somewhat neglected fact, that the salmon caught at that spot were all on their way up to him.—ED.

and nibble at it as they please, but still the principle stands firm as a rock. That the Crown has been in the practice of making grants of servitudes to coast heritors to intercept the salmon *passing* on to the rivers, can add nothing to their legality, since no practice can render that legal which is in itself otherwise. So has the Crown been in the practice of granting the coast heritors rights to *yairs*, which are declared (even those of the Crown itself) by repeated Acts of Parliament to be *illegal*, and the mere fact of their being granted by the Crown cannot render them otherwise; yet the Court of·Session, which, as we have said, seldom troubles itself with principles, has been in the habit of considering these yair grants as legal, and it is therefore the less wonder that they should look on the grants of the servitudes upon the rivers to be so.

If these servitudes of intercepting the fish passing on to the rivers cannot be defended without violating a great principle of law, the claims of the coast heritors will not acquire much strength on the score of *justice;* for, exclusive of what we have already said, that there is no possible connection between their *lands* and the salmon in a different element, let us just look to the manner in which their grants have been obtained. For example, a possessor of land on the coast, some fifty or a hundred years ago, takes it into his head that he could catch salmon opposite to his lands, and applies to the Crown for a fishing grant, as a bagatelle, to be obtained for asking. The Crown, however, lest any existing vested right should be injured thereby, renders the application public by advertisement, and if no objection be made, taking it for granted that no injury could arise from it to any, the grant is given, *gratis*, as asked. The grant, after being thus obtained, is found, however, to be useless, and becomes a dead letter in the titles of the lands, so that if the estate is sold, not one farthing is paid for fishings which have no actual existence, and which pay no rent. In the mean time stake-nets are invented, and all the grants immediately start into life. These engines, placed on the course of the salmon, open a prospect of *intercepting* nearly the whole of them on their way to the rivers, and of transferring the fishery to the coasts. Unfortunately, the ancient statutes interpose their protection, and the coast heritors, who, as we have said, never paid one farthing for their fishings, exclaim, What *injustice !* Only think of the hardship, the cruelty, of being thus prevented from appropriating to ourselves the properties of the river heritors, which, having always paid rents, were purchased many of them at high prices, and have been possessed for time immemorial, just as we have possessed our lands. Here the Sovereign might tell them, You got your grants under the idea that they would do no harm to other properties—why else do you suppose your applications were rendered public by advertisement? and rest assured, that the motive from which *that* was done, would, had stake-nets been foreseen, have prevented the grants being given at all. You must, therefore, fish according to the *usage* of the fishery at the period the grants were made, for long usage constitutes law ; and you have no right to use the grants for the purpose of spoliation, and transferring properties to yourselves, which were never intended to be given to you. Certes, in every view the clamour of the coast heritors is ridiculous, as well as unjust ; but they have received a degree of support from the courts of law, which has in many instances proved most disastrous to the river fishings. A volume would scarcely contain all the acts of *injustice* which we could relate on the subject, since the introduction of *fixed* nets into the fishery. The greatest depredations have been committed on the established fisheries, from a dependence by the depredators on the *delays* of the law, regardless of what the event might be, provided the produce of the fishery could, in the mean time, be carried off. Illegal spoliation of property became, in short, a legal speculation—fostered by the conduct of the Court in refusing interdicts—as if there could be any hardship in forcing parties to continue the *usage* of the fishery until the legality of the new modes of fishing, that is, of the new fishing-engines, which can never, in *any* instance, be permitted without injustice, should be ascertained.

The salmon-fishery now constitutes so large a portion of the property of Scotland, and the law on the subject seems to be so ill understood, every new case which occurs undergoing the same tedious course of litigation, as if the judges were groping their way in the dark, at a loss, amid clouds of mystification, supported often by the most barefaced falsehoods, how to act, that we think it would be of vast service to the country if one judge were set apart for fishing cases, whose legal knowledge, all bent upon one object, would soon have added to it so thorough a knowledge of the true nature of the fishery, as would enable him to render the law clear on the subject, and, by reducing the whole to fixed principles, would prevent the absurdities and the anomalies which now daily occur. His remarks and reports would be most valuable, not merely with reference to the rights of parties, but with a view to the improvement of the fishery as regards the public, while they would save a world of expense in litigation, and much fishing property from destruction. At present the fishery may be said to be absolutely without legal protection, save in the Tay, as if the statutes were framed for that estuary alone. In short, the whole fishing system seems to be in a state of general and absolute confusion—a state, perhaps, the best possible for the lawyers and agents, but which parties, from the one end of the kingdom to the other, look to with dismay.

Hitherto it has been considered the law, that without a Crown grant (whether legal or otherwise) salmon-fishing operations could not be legally carried on anywhere; but, amid all the improvements in the fishery, it is now found, that even this may be dispensed with, and that the salmon may be taken in all parts without a grant; in other words, the fishery, hitherto limited to the Crown's grantees, has been thrown open to universal spoliation. The cases wherein this *new* law has been declared, the most important, perhaps, in principle, after the decisions in the Tay and Kintore cases, which has taken place for a century, ought to be generally known, and, when known, will be scarcely believed, so contrary is the principle—so unguardedly and unfortunately laid down, to the common rules of justice.

Mackenzie, proprietor of the river Shinn, in Sutherlandshire, one of the four salmon-rivers which, combined, form the freshwater estuary, called by Boethius, and other ancient writers, the River of Portnacoulter, now termed by some the Kyle of

Sutherland, by others the Frith of Dornoch, and which is, in fact, a collection of fresh water, or of conjoined rivers, subject to the influx of the tide, or a great tide river—and tenant or tacksman of nearly the whole of the rivers and upper fishings, paying high rents, and supporting expensive fishing establishments, was lately forced, after all remonstrance had failed, to raise an action against Houston, possessor of some land, called Creich, on the estuary, for intercepting the salmon proceeding to the rivers, at a part where the channel of the estuary, at low water, was one-third less in breadth than the Thames at Westminster bridge, without having either a Crown grant, or a prescriptive right, or, in short, a right of any kind, which could authorise him to do so. Houston admitted the absence of all right on his part, but contended that, if he had not a right, the right, that is, the right of interception, was in the Crown, or in some one else, and denied the title of the pursuer, as an upper heritor, to raise the action; but this defence was *unanimously* rejected by the Second Division of the Court, the title of the pursuer, as an upper heritor, sustained, and Houston found liable in expenses, which put an end to the case.

In the meanwhile, Houston's immediate neighbour, Gilchrist, who had lately acquired right to a small spot called Spinningdale, on the banks of the estuary, lately belonging to a cotton-spinning manufactory, commenced similar proceedings, without any right. Another action was accordingly raised against him, when the same defence was resorted to, namely, the want of *title* in the pursuer, as an upper heritor to pursue. This case having come before the Ordinary of the other, or First Division of the Court, his Lordship pronounced an interlocutor directly the REVERSE of the one in the former case, finding, that the pursuer, as an upper heritor, had NOT a title to raise the action, unless he could produce a right to the very *spot* where the interception took place, or show that the fish were intercepted by an illegal *engine*, the matter, that is, the interception of the fish and consequent loss of property, being, his Lordship said, wholly *jus tertii* to the upper heritors; and the man who was fraudulently transferring to himself what, by his own avowal, he had no right to, was found entitled to his expenses from the person he was robbing—the *bond fide* grantee of the Crown, all which was confirmed by his Lordship's Division of the Court.

Here we have two judgments of the Court, on precisely the *same* point, directly in the teeth of each other. Which of them, then, was LAW? If the law was clear on the subject, how happened the whole of the judges of the Second Division of the Court, whose contrary decision, as we said, was *unanimous*, to be utterly ignorant of it? The question was, in fact, a very simple one—viz. Whether a person, who complains of injury, or loss of property, from the acts of one who, by his own confession, had no right to inflict such injury, had a title to seek redress? The one Division of the Court were unanimous that he had, the other that he had NOT; and as the latter prevailed, the sufferer was found liable in expenses, for making the attempt, to the person whom it was not once pretended had a right to inflict the injury. The opinion by which the Court were led was, that the Crown *might*, if it chose, inflict the injury complained of, and as the Crown might do it, the defender, who only did what the Crown *might* do, could only be punished by the Crown for doing it; and this miserable QUIBBLING was held out as *law*, for the purpose, as we have said, of enabling a man to appropriate to himself what he had no right to.

It could not, however, be very agreeable to the Court that these contradictory judgments, on the same point, should remain, in the face of each other, upon the records. What would the country think of it? What would future lawyers say? What opinion would they form of the Court? Which decision would hereafter be considered law, the one in accordance with *justice*, or the one which disregarded and trampled upon justice? Then the legal reputation of the two divisions of the Court was brought into unfortunate collision. Which of the two divisions must succumb? All this was undoubtedly most mortifying; but *que faire?* So, to end the matter, Houston's agent, a man of excellent *tact*, if scrimp of brains, kindly brought his case again into the Second Division, and though the judgment had become final from the lapse of time, or what lawyers term a *res judicata,* and though not one single new argument was advanced, the Court reversed their former unanimous decision, and found Houston, in his turn, entitled to expenses!

When we saw this decision, in which it was found that the interception of the fish passing on to the upper fishings gave the upper heritors no title to complain, unless they could show a right, on their own part, to the very *spot* where the fish were intercepted, we were led to suppose that salmon had been considered as *fixed* to the ground, like oysters, so that, to entitle a man to raise an action, he must have a right to the ground to which they are fixed; or, when the matter was declared to be *jus tertii* to the upper heritors, that it was believed the salmon fell into the rivers and upper fisheries direct from the clouds, as the wise *Olaus Magnus* tells us the rats, or lemmings, do in Lapland, and consequently that the interception of the fish in the estuary could do the upper heritors no harm; but then this would be at variance with the part of the interlocutor which declares that the title of the upper heritors would be good if they could show that the salmon were intercepted by an illegal *engine,* which was an admission that they were really on their way to the rivers, and did not fall into them like the Lapland rats of the wise *Olaus Magnus.* The upshot of the doctrine is, that an illegal *mode* of fishing gives a title to pursue, but that the illegal *act* of fishing without a right does not. Can anybody understand this legal distinction between an illegal MODE and an illegal ACT of fishing, as constituting a *title* to pursue? To us it appears very like nonsense. It is one of those niceties, so very nice, as to defy common sense to comprehend it; but what shall we say of the *justice* of the country, when a distinction, which carries absurdity on the face of it, is laid hold of to shelter injustice? To defeat a title, and thus prevent a competition of rights which could not stand a moment's hearing? It must be clear to common sense that, if a man has a title to pursue for the interception of the fish by an illegal engine, his title must be equally good to pursue for their interception by a poacher—a person without a right. It is no wonder if men of plain sense exclaim, Such are the *mysteries* of the law! what fine-spun brains those lawyers must have! we cannot comprehend them. And truly nonsense is a mystery which is not easily comprehended. We suppose the argument means something like this: if a man knocks another on the head, the knockee will have no title to complain of the knocker, unless he can show that the knock was given with an illegal *weapon*. In the same way, if a man should steal, or appropriate to his own use, a sheep on its way to another man's farm, to which he himself had no right (and when a man appropriates to himself what he has no right to, it looks very like stealing, or at least is brother-german to theft), under pretence that though HE had no right to it, the parson might, if he chose, take it as his tithe, or his Majesty might take it, if he pleased, for taxes. Scotch law would tell the farmer, " the man, it is true, had no right to the sheep, and you have suffered a loss by his taking it; but as the parson or the king *might* have taken it, they only can pursue him for doing so, unless, indeed, you can show that it was carried off in an illegal way; for instance, in an illegal sack, that is, a sack made of contraband stuff, for that would give you a good *title* to pursue, which the loss you have suffered, or the loss of your whole property, would not." *Que tout cela est beau*, quoth the farmer; *Vive la Justice!*

Every judge knows, or ought to know, that the only difference which there can be between an illegal engine and the usual mode of fishing, *quoad* the upper heritors, as the lawyers say, is that the one intercepts a greater number of the passing fish than another. An illegal engine may intercept 150 salmon, while a common net will only take 100. The difference is, therefore, only in degree, and this degree of difference must constitute the title to pursue, for the mere *illegality* of the engine would, of itself, give no title to pursue, since, if placed on land, the upper heritors would have no title to object to what did them no harm. Some reason in common sense should have been given why the additional 50 salmon intercepted by illegal machinery should constitute a title, while the same number intercepted by the carcase of a poacher does not. We conceive the one engine to be just as illegal, on the point in question, as the other. The illegality of the engine alone,

Scotch law says, does not constitute a title, and the taking of the fish alone does not constitute a title ; separately, they are innocuous—quite harmless—useless ; but, united, they form a good title, just as two ciphers, when added together, make an unit, or two blanks a prize. Such is the *law* brought into existence by the opinions of judges, and by which the most valuable property of individuals is disposed of.

If we were to ask what has made this LAW, we believe any judge would be somewhat puzzled to inform us. If he were to tell us candidly the truth, he would say, "that which makes nine-tenths of our law the mere accidental opinion of the judge." When the legislature makes a law, there is debate upon debate, it is canvassed in all its parts, viewed in every light, must pass through both Houses, and acquire the final sanction of the King: but a judge saves himself all this trouble ; in five minutes he makes a law at once ; declares any vague idea which comes across his brain to be LAW ; and the one law is just as effectual for the disposal of property as the other. It is a pity, possessed of such despotic power, that where there is not clear law, the judge does not always extract law from the feeling or sentiment of *justice*. But the vulgar instinct of justice is common to all men, and excites no admiration, while a legal subtlety shows the acuteness of the mind of the judge. Besides, if law were always founded in justice and common sense (we mean the law dealt out to us, for *sound* law is ever so), it would lose that mysteriousness, that charlatanism in which it is enveloped, and which creates the wonderment of the people. It is therefore necessary to show up the magic-lantern, to keep the country in a state of delusion, and to add to the dignity of the judge. In this respect the interest of the legal profession and of the people is in direct opposition to each other. It is the interest of the people that law should be rendered as simple, and justice as certain as possible ; it is surely not the interest of judges to perplex the law, in order to retain their darling POWER over property, though it may be of the lawyers in order to increase litigation—which, if *justice* were invariably to take place, would be reduced to one-half its present extent. Accordingly, justice, as we said before, is in little repute in our Courts, and law is everything. Every case which comes into Court is made to turn upon some sophism, or subtlety, or nicety, or chimerical distinction of what is called law ; and justice, the end and object of law, the very thing for which law has been made, and with which, as we have before observed, *sound* law is never at variance, is utterly disregarded ; of which the case before us, with the quibbling distinction, between an illegal *mode* and an illegal *act* of fishing, and still more quibbling assertion, that what the Crown may do, all others may also do, is a clear instance.

When the case came before the Court, we would have expected that, instead of having recourse to such quibbles, it would have been said to the defender, " Sir, the river heritors hold their properties by grants from the Crown, and under these grants they have been in the immemorial possession of the whole of the fish which pass up through the channel of the estuary : you wish to appropriate to yourself a portion of these fish, of which they have been in immemorial possession, while you admit that YOU have no *right* to them. A man who appropriates to himself what he has no right to, commits an act of THEFT, be it on whom it may. If the salmon belong to the Crown, he steals the property of the Crown ; if to the Crown's grantees, he steals their property. In either view, he is to every intent and purpose a thief, and this is what you wish us judges to protect you in. If, as Erskine states, the fish constitute the *estate* of the owners of the fishings, it would be a great absurdity to say that they have no right of property in what constitutes their estate. There is not a salmon taken by you, which, if not so taken, the tacksman of the upper fisheries would not be as sure of as if it were in his ice-house.* You take what may belong professedly to the Crown, but what is substantially, or, in FACT, the property of the owners of the fishery ; but, in either view, you take what does not belong to YOU. Sitting here as judges, bound by our OATHS, to adminis-

---

* We once tied a bit of tape round the tail of a fish taken at a lower fishery, and allowed it to escape—and sent off a man immediately to one of the upper rivers to which we knew it belonged, but before the man reached the river, the fish was caught there, with the tape about it.

ter justice as well as law, we cannot sanction your conduct. We cannot consider, as *law*, a quibble which has, on the very face of it, and by your own showing, no other object than to cover *theft;* and it would be contrary to all justice to allow you, and if you, all others, to appropriate to yourselves, without a right, what had been possessed for time immemorial, by the owners of the rivers under their grants from the Crown—to allow you, by your united efforts, in fact, to deprive them of their properties altogether. Every principle of honour, of justice, of *sound* law, and even of morality, forbids it ; and when a judge loses all sense of morality, and covers an act of dishonesty by a trick, he loses all title to respect. Go home, then, sir, and be satisfied with what you have a *right* to, without appropriating to yourself what you have *not* a right to. Learn a lesson of honesty : at all events expect not that we will do your dirty work for you." But no judge said this : moral judges, who could put on black caps to sentence to the gallows the unfortunate criminal, pressed, perhaps, by necessity, to appropriate to himself what he had no right to, appear unintentionally to shield the *same* offence in another, by a miserable quibble, and even find him entitled to COSTS! Accordingly, the tacksman of the upper fisheries is told, " The Crown might, if it pleased, deprive you of all the fish—of your property—of your vested rights : and if the Crown could do it, so may the defender, for the defender does nothing but what the Crown *might* do, if it pleased. You have no redress : you must put up with your loss : you cannot help yourself : the loss of your property is a matter wholly *jus tertii* to you, with which you have no manner of concern : such is the *law*, which is the essence of *justice.*" Now, suppose our tacksman were disposed to return to the inventor a dose of his own law, and, aided by a posse of his fishermen, as a press-gang, were to carry him on board one of his Majesty's tenders, in Leith Roads, and then say to him, " His Majesty has a right to impress men into his service as seamen ; I have done nothing to you but what his Majesty *might* do if he pleased, and his Majesty alone can find fault with me for it. You have no redress : you cannot help yourself : the matter is wholly *jus tertii* to YOU. Such is the law, and the law, you say, is the essence of justice. A voyage to New South Wales will do you a vast deal of good, and will give you leisure to ruminate on all the *consequences* of the law of *jus tertii*, as laid down by yourself, and now brought home to you. Good-by, mon cher: portez vous bien. If you find any salmon in New South Wales, you will probably think of your friend, the *jus tertii* tacksman."

If a man were to cut down and carry off, or steal a tree from one of his Majesty's forests, the act would no doubt be truly *jus tertii* to all others, except his Majesty, because to no others could it do any injury; though, even in this case, there would be no great room to admire the *morals* of the court, who would attempt to screen the offence, by the absurd quibble that because his Majesty himself might, if he pleased, cut the tree, all others might do so too; but granting that the quibble, for it can scarcely be called a principle, because it is contrary to every principle of common sense, did apply to this case, still it could not be made to extend to cases where an actual injury was inflicted on others, by depriving them of property for time immemorial possessed. If, as we have just stated, on the authority of Erskine, the salmon constitute the *estate* of the Crown's fishing grantees, as much as the land constitutes the estate of the Crown's land grantees, it must, as we said, be a great absurdity to maintain that they have not a right of *property* in such estate, or that the very article which he says *constitutes* their estate, should *still* belong to the Crown, because it once did so. To deny their title, therefore, to prosecute those who deprive them of such estate, is the very highest degree of injustice; for if the salmon do not constitute the estate, what does so? Perhaps we may be told, in the hackneyed style, to which we have already alluded, that in making the grants to the river heritors, the Crown only gave them a right to *catch* salmon there. Let any lawyer show us, if he can, a grant in which the word "catch" is inserted—and if he cannot, where is his authority for saying it? He may say, that in granting all the mills in the kingdom, the Crown granted only a right to *grind* in them; but would the mere circumstance of his saying so, or thinking so, or the idea having come into his head, be considered proof of it, or make it *law?* We have already remarked, that if salmon were like haddocks, which seems to be the notion entertained of them by some judges, the Crown could only give a right to " catch" them, because haddocks do not admit, from their nature, to become property; but, to return to our former illustration of pigeons belonging to their cots, which is so applicable to salmon belonging to their rivers, if the Crown granted to a man the pigeons of a certain dove-cot, would any honest lawyer maintain that the Crown only granted him a right to "catch" them, and gave no right of property in them, or that, notwithstanding having so granted them away, they still belong to the Crown? To argue upon a grant of pigeons, as if they were like larks or thrushes, or regarding salmon as if they were like haddocks, or, in short, regarding any one animal, not as it actually is, or upon its *own* nature, but upon the nature of other animals, can never, in any instance, as we before remarked, lead but to error; and this, as we have already stated, has been the grand cause of so much error regarding salmon, which are viewed, not as they actually are, *belonging* to the rivers, the right to which was just as much a right of property as a right to the pigeons *belonging* to their respective cots, but as haddocks, which belong to no particular part, and to which, therefore, no right of property could, as we said, be affixed. But, setting all argument on the subject aside, the very FACT stated by Erskine, and obvious to all, that the fish constitute the *estate* of the grantees, from which a right of property CANNOT be separated, is conclusive on the subject. It is a point which cannot be got over.

That the Crown, in granting the river fisheries, *reserved* a right to impose servitudes upon them, of intercepting the fish in their way to them, we have repeatedly denied—for there is no such reservation, as we have said, inserted in the grants, and it would be absurd to say it could be *implied* with regard to salmon-rivers, any more than with regard to lands. The single circumstance we have already stated, that such servitudes might be so multiplied along the coasts as to occasion the utter eviction of the river fisheries, is *alone* a sufficient refutation of such doctrine. But even if the Crown had the power of creating such servitudes, still it is evident that they do not exist, and cannot exist, until the Crown creates them, or brings them into existence; could anything, therefore, be more absurd than to say, that Houston was exercising, in the room of the Crown, a right of fishing, which the Crown had not yet created, or brought into existence?

Let the owners of the salmon-rivers in Scotland only look at the *consequences* of the law, as laid down in this case, and unfortunately affirmed recently in the Court of Appeal. A man may have been possessed, under a grant from the Crown, of a salmon-fishing in a river, for time immemorial, with a free and unobstructed run to the fish from the mouth of the river to his fishing; and not only, we are told, may the Crown, notwithstanding his immemorial possession, but his immediate neighbour below him, who has no right of fishing, may NOW, without any authority from the Crown, sweep the whole river in front of his fishing, within a few yards of it, and absolutely extinguish it, and he will have no *title* to prevent him. Even a man possessed of only ten furlongs or ten yards of land, worth not perhaps five shillings a-year, near the mouth of a river, may intercept the whole of the fish as they enter, and thus ruin the fishery of the river; and though unpossessed of a particle of legal right, may transfer to himself the whole fishing property of the river, worth perhaps £500 or £1500 a-year, and the legal owner, thus robbed of his property, will have no title to prevent it. In the same way, should a parcel of fishermen form themselves into a gang, and have wherewith to purchase nets, they may, as a fishing speculation, in consequence of this new law, sweep the whole waters in front of the established fisheries, from one end of the kingdom to the other, and if they pay a trifle to the owners of lands, to prevent molestation on their part, neither the owners nor the tacksmen of the fisheries will have a title to prevent them. In short, all protection is at once removed from fishing property all over Scotland.

That such law, which carries the grossest injustice on the face of it, should be affirmed in the Court of Appeal, and affirmed, too, by such a man as Lord Brougham, is to us of all things the most astonishing*—and can only be accounted for, by supposing that the case was not laid before his lordship in its proper light; for we cannot permit ourselves to believe, for one moment, that, if it had been fully explained, this would have been the case. We entertain the highest possible respect for the Court of Appeal. Its judgments are almost always founded in correct principles, and the mind of the judge is invariably *pure;* but if cases are not fully developed, and placed in their proper light, error, the lot of fallible man, *must* sometimes find its way into the judgment, though we believe that in no Court on earth does it do so more seldom; and of all cases which can come into the Court, there are none so liable to misconstruction and error as those which regard the salmon fishery, for there are none which either the judge or the counsel, or even the agents, can be expected, from their nature, to be so little acquainted with. An occasional error, in a fishing case, seems therefore, in an English Court, scarcely avoidable; but we have not the least doubt that when such is discovered, the candour and the love of justice by which all noble minds are distinguished, will lead the highly gifted individual who presides in that Court to take the earliest opportunity of rectifying it. In the mean time, however, its effects must be fatally disastrous to many individuals, and to many fisheries, and the sooner, therefore, another case of the same kind is brought under the view of the Court the better. That the judgment is founded in a wrong principle there cannot be a doubt, because that CANNOT be a right principle which enables one man to rob another of his property, under the pretence that a third person *might* do so; but unless it was explained to the judge that such would be the effect of the principle, which we understand was *not* done in the case in question, how was he to know it? How, unacquainted personally with the subject, was he to know the extent of spoliation to which the principle would lead? That all salmon-fishings emanate from the Crown is true; and so, as we said before, do all lands; but both can be now only considered as *private property*, entitled to the same legal protection. With

* September 13, 1831.

regard to the rights of the Crown, whatever they may be, it is time enough to try the point when a question with the Crown arises, and which it was entirely and truly *jus tertii* in Houston or any other to institute.

The maxim, then, that there can be no wrong without redress, is an error ; since it is now openly and publicly established as LAW by the highest tribunal in the kingdom, founded in a quibble, that not only may a wrong, and a great wrong, be committed with impunity, but that a man may be even deprived of his whole property by another who has no right to it, and that he will have NO TITLE TO REDRESS.

But to continue Houston's case in the Court of Session. When the honest man found that the Court was so well disposed towards him, he judged that he might even venture a little farther, and make hay while the sun shined. He had hitherto fished only in the usual way, or with the movable coble-net ; but he now planted *fixed* or bag nets, which we have already described as the most destructive of all fishing engines, in the very *alveus* or channel of the water, or passage of the fish to the upper fisheries, and which but few fish could escape. A new complaint from the tacksman to the Court was necessarily the consequence of this new aggression, but the Court heard him with the utmost apathy, and would not listen to a word he could say on the subject. The interdict which they had granted in a similar case in the Tay,[*] they *refused* to him, and allowed the man who had no right to fish, or to intercept the fish in *any* way, not only to sweep the channel with movable nets, but even to fill it with the most destructive fixed machinery, with engines which they themselves had interdicted in situations far less destructive elsewhere ; and to continue his operations during the season. How can this refusal of all legal protection, granted to others, be then justified, except by supposing unacquaintance with the subject of the salmon-fishing ? Did the Court suppose that the fish could go through Houston's nets to the upper fisheries ? Or was the quality of the water their reason for it ? The water at the part in question is in general quite fresh, and never more than brackish, corresponding exactly with the Thames at

[*] Duke of Athol *v.* Wedderburne, 16th December 1826.

Woolwich; but let it be what it might, were it as salt as the ocean, could that justify so gross an act of *injustice* to the whole upper fisheries as to allow the passage of the fish, only 178 yards in breadth, the only way by which they could reach them, to be blocked up with *fixed machinery*, which must be deemed illegal, and a nuisance in *common law*, were the fishing statutes, or the supposed quality of the water to which they allude, not in existence? The whole of the salmon of the four upper rivers must necessarily pass through this narrow channel, of the breadth we have described; and yet the Court, guided by their new law founded on ignorance of the nature of the fishery, not only allow a man (who has no right, even by his own avowal) to sweep the channel with movable nets, but even to plant it with fixed machinery, leaving the upper heritors and their tacksman, with his rents and fishing establishments, to their fate.

SECTION V.

SCOTTISH STATUTES.

Ceux qui se sont fait un métier de la chicane ne peuvent avoir l'esprit juste et éclairé.   ROCHEFOUCAULT.

WE have just remarked, that the grants by the Crown of salmon-fishings to the proprietors of lands situated on the coasts, being made in direct violation of an acknowledged great principle of the law, must necessarily be illegal; the whole salmon-fishing rights of the Crown being, in fact, exhausted when the rivers were granted, so that nothing remained to the Crown to give; and the Crown could therefore give nothing, except by taking away, by interception, what had been already granted to the owners of the rivers, and had become their vested right, as much as any landed estate in the kingdom is so. But even were this *not* the case, still the use of fixed engines in coast fisheries is prohibited in Scotland by the Statutes, which in this respect have come in aid of *justice*. By the usage of the salmon-fishery,—and we believe long *usage* alone constitutes law, when not contrary to any legal enactments,—the whole fishery was, as we have said, carried on by net and coble. Now many salmon will pass the movable coble-net; even in the act of hauling it in, the fish pass on to the adjacent fishery; but if a *fixed* net were placed in front of such fishery, it would extinguish it at once. This power of extinguishing an adjacent fishery we conceive to be utterly illegal in PRINCIPLE, and ought alone to be sufficient to condemn the fixed-net system in all parts; for no system can be legal which lays the property of one man at the mercy of another. If, by the usage of the coble and net, coast fishings were of little value, the owners of them, in purchasing their properties, paid as little for them : and if they paid nothing for *ideal* fishings, illegal in the very Grants, and which in most cases had no actual existence, is it just that they should be allowed, by new fishing machinery, to extinguish, or to transfer to themselves, the properties of their neighbours—properties which are in every respect as much entitled to legal protection as their own lands, or any other species of property? A man may improve, as we have already remarked, a land estate without any injury to others, but he *cannot* improve his salmon-fishery—in a part where others have rights—by new fishing engines, without occasioning a corresponding diminution of their fisheries; and this we conceive to be an unanswerable reason, in justice, why the *usage* of the fishery by net and coble, under which the whole fishing properties were acquired or purchased, should not be departed from.

When stake-nets were introduced into the estuary of the Tay, the upper heritors, however, whose fisheries were threatened with being rendered utterly useless by the interception of the fish, and which had in fact declined exactly in proportion to the increase in the number of the stake-nets, as has been already shown, instead of proceeding against these engines on the ground of the common law, founded on the *usage* of the fishery, or upon the mere plain principles of *justice*, either of which ought to have been quite sufficient for their purpose, had recourse to certain ancient *Statutes* of the Scottish Legislature, by which yairs and similar engines are prohibited "in waters where the tide ebbs and flows, as destructive of the fry of all fishes."

We shall not trace all the lengthened course of litigation which took place in this celebrated Case, which occupied the attention of the Court of Session for so long a period of time. It was, in truth, a Case of mere quibbling and sophistication from one end to the other. Great lawyers made fine speeches, replete with eloquence and with nonsense, which, as is often the case, left the matter in greater obscurity than they found it. The meaning of the word "Water," in the statutes, was a puzzle of the very worst kind. Did it mean waters in general, or only rivers ? This was a sad point, which it took *fourteen long years* to determine. Both the Judges and the Counsel, no doubt, did their best, in the way in which they handle all the cases which come before them. The Judges quoted old songs, and the counsel cited the classics—Ovid, Virgil, and Horace—to show the intentions of those ancient worthies, the Scotch Legislators, in framing their fishing Statutes, until at length, by their united efforts, they made *nonsense* of the Statutes, and then most unjustly laid the blame—not upon themselves, and their absurd constructions, but upon the defunct legislators.

If the Court had only read these statutes like other Acts of Parliament, and as we conceive all Acts of the Legislature intended *for the guidance of the lieges* ought to be read—in short, in the only way which a Court of Law has a *right* to read them, namely, in the plain common-sense meaning of the words—they would have found them as consistent and intelligible, and as full of good sense, as any Acts in the Statute Book. But this would not satisfy the Scotch Court; any man might do that—they must do something more—they must see difficulties where none existed—put constructions upon words the reverse of what in their natural sense they bore, and discover intentions in the ancient Legislators which never entered into their heads, else where would be their superiority over others ? Besides, as we said before, plain common-sense seems to be held in utter contempt where quibbles, and sophisms, and subtleties, and chimerical distinctions are alone attended to. This we cannot too often repeat, because it cannot be too often impressed upon the Scotch public, who are gulled with what is *called* law, and denied JUSTICE. The Court accordingly declared that the prohibitions in the statutes were intended by the Legislature to be confined to *rivers*, or fresh waters, and they held and still hold out this as LAW—the law of the statutes—and daily decide upon questions of fishing property by this law. Now, without any disrespect to the Court, which we hold, as in duty bound, in high reverence, we *deny* that this is the law ; we maintain that it is NOT the law of the statutes, but law of the Court of Session's own making, in direct opposition to the statutes. We assert that the Court have *altered* the meaning of the statutes—have done what none but the Legislature has a right to do—have substituted a law of *their own* in the room of the law of the statutes, which even the affirmation of the Court of Appeal cannot convert into law, since nothing can legally do so save an Act of Parliament. All the decisions, therefore, which have taken place upon this supposed law—this perversion of the statutes—must be deemed illegal, unless it be admitted that the Court of Session possess legally the power, which it unquestionably often assumes, of *making* law—that is, of declaring its own sentiments to be law; and good enough law too, perhaps, it may be said, for the country that could so long submit to it, without petitioning the Legislature for reform of such abuses.

The ground upon which the Court has declared that the prohibition of fixed engines in the statutes was intended to apply only to rivers, is their construction of the word "Waters," which, after fourteen years of deliberation, as we said, it has asserted, means fresh waters or rivers—an assertion which is directly contradicted by every expression in the statutes themselves. The only mention of rivers or fresh waters in the statutes, is where cruives are expressly *allowed* there, though prohibited in all other parts. It is quite clear that the word "Waters" was used either in its *general* sense, as applying to all waters, or in its more confined sense, as denoting rivers, a sense in which it is often used in the technical language in the titles to Scotch estates. If the expression was deemed ambiguous, instead of looking for explanation in the classics, we think the better way would have been to look for it in the statutes themselves. The first, or model statute (Robert I.), from which all the subsequent statutes seem to have been framed, says, " In *Aquis ubi ascendit mare et se retrahit, et ubi salmunculi, vel smelti, sui friæ alterius generis piscium* maris vel aquæ dulcis," &c. That is, in waters where the fry of *sea* fishes, or of fresh-water fishes, or of *any* kind of fish, are to be found. Now, does the Court of Session suppose that the fry of SEA fishes, or of all fishes, are *only* to be found in fresh-water rivers? Can there be a more direct contradiction than the words fry of *sea* fishes, or of all fishes, which are never found in rivers or fresh waters, and which could not live there a day, to the assertion of the Court, that the word "waters" was intended to be restricted to rivers or fresh waters,—and that it was not used in its *general* sense, as applying to waters of every description, where the fry of sea fishes, or of all fishes, or of *any* kind or description of fish, are to be found and could be destroyed? We do not think that it was possible to express the prohibition in terms more *general* or comprehensive. Yairs could only be placed where the *tide* ebbs and flows; and the statutes therefore prohibit them in "all waters within reach of the *tide;*" that is, in all parts where they could be placed, or where fry of *any* kind, whether of sea or river fishes, could be destroyed. But the Court of Session says this only means rivers, where yairs could *not* be erected, and where the fry of sea fishes are *not* to be found. The statutes describe these yairs as *actually* destroying the fry of all fishes; and the Court of Session tells us this must mean rivers, which the fry of all fishes never enter! Some of the statutes expressly mention the prohibition to be in *salt* water that ebbs and flows, where the fry of all fishes are truly and actually destroyed by yairs, as the statutes state; the fry of sea fishes swimming about the shores, and the fry of salmon in their descent from the rivers: but the Court of Session says that salt water *means* fresh water, because it is in fresh water *only* the fry of sea fishes can be destroyed; and this perfect *nonsense* it assures the country is LAW—the law of the statutes—and dispose of the most valuable vested rights of individuals, as we said, accordingly. If Lord Lyndhurst, from want of proper explanation, or of due consideration, acceded to the opinion of the Court in the Kintore Case,* that assuredly (however this individual case may have been disposed of by it) does not constitute it LAW, contrary to the plain meaning of the statutes— since nothing, as we said before, can legally do so save an Act of Parliament.

* This is the first case we have ever seen decided in the Court of Appeal on grounds of absolute nonsense.

The object of the Scottish Legislature in framing the statutes is obvious. In those remote periods of time, Scotland, always poor from her soil and climate, possessed no article for export trade save the produce of her fisheries, which nature bestowed liberally on her, to make up for her other wants. Of these fisheries, salmon formed, undoubtedly, a part; but it is clear that the herring and white-fish fisheries were the most important in a public or national view; the care of the Legislature, however, extended equally to both, and, indeed, to the preservation of the fry of every kind of fish around their coasts, as the whole of the statutes show. Even in later times, in the preamble to an Act of Queen Anne, it is said, "Our Sovereign Lady and Estates of Parliament, taking it into consideration the great many advantages that may arise to this nation by encouraging the *salmon, white and herring, fisheries,* they *being not only a certain fund to advance the trade and increase the wealth* thereof, but also a true and ready way to breed seamen, and set many poor and idle people to work," &c.

Now, of all the engines by which fry could be destroyed, yairs were by far the most destructive. They consisted of a long range of stakes, with wattling, somewhat resembling a hedge, carried from the land into the sea to low-water mark, in the form of a crescent—with a *croe*, or cruive, in the centre, and a curve or horn at the extremity. These engines, like the present stake-nets, were always placed on the coasts of friths or of the sea, in parts where the tide left the sands dry at low water to a great extent; for so simple was their construction, that nowhere else could they be of any use. Thus Mr Little states in the Committee—"Yairs could not fish but in the TIDE." The *tide* was, therefore, the *sine quâ non* of all such erections, and hence, as we said, the prohibition in the statutes of these engines "where the TIDE ebbs and flows." In general, they were used more as a matter of convenience than of profit, by affording a constant supply, at every ebb-tide, of small sea-fishes, as flounders, sea-trout, cuddies, and occasionally a few herrings and salmon; but they were, in every instance, most destructive of the fry of all fishes, floating about the coasts in the easy water near the shore; and, among the rest, of the fry of salmon in their descent from the rivers. In the Tay case it was attempted to be proved, by theorists and jobbers, that the salmon-fry on leaving the rivers plunge into deep water—but the FACT of their being caught in yairs on the coasts shows the contrary.

No yairs ever were attempted to be placed in *rivers* in Scotland, because there are no situations within the banks of Scotch rivers where they could be erected, or where, if erected, they would not be swept away by the first flood in the river; and yet it is where they *could not* be erected—where they never were *attempted* to be erected, and where the fry "of all fishes" are *never found*—that the Court of Session declare the ancient Legislature passed act after act to prevent their being erected, which is not consistent with common sense. The only mention, as before observed, in the statutes of rivers or fresh waters, is for the purpose of regulating the cruives which were expressly *allowed* there, directing that the hecks should be three inches wide, which will allow a salmon of *ten* pounds to pass through. With the same width of hecks, cruives could not obstruct the passage of fry *anywhere*, yet they are prohibited by the statutes in all parts except in the rivers—the very part to which the Court, reversing the meaning of the statutes, say the prohibitions do apply—the desire of the Legislature being evidently to keep the coasts clear of all standing machinery, in the way of either the fry or of the salmon returning to the rivers, else why, when cruives were allowed in the rivers, should they have been prohibited elsewhere? No man will allege that hecks which would allow a salmon of ten pounds to pass through them, could be injurious to fry along the coasts, any more than in the rivers, where they are expressly allowed: the prohibition of them elsewhere could therefore only arise, as we have just said, from a determination in the Legislature to keep the coasts clear of all fixed machinery whatever; and when we consider the manner in which the salmon-shoals, when coming on to the rivers, are broken and dispersed by such machinery on the coasts, we cannot but admire the knowledge and sagacity with which the various enactments were made, both with regard to them and the fry.

Hence Sir H. Davy remarked to the Committee, that by the ancient Scottish law, salmon-fishings were never considered to belong to the *coasts*.

The species of machinery called yairs, which were the forerunners of the stake-nets, and which, as we said, were invariably placed, and could only be placed, on the coasts of friths and the sea, actually destroyed immense quantities of the fry of all fishes, as the statutes state. The herrings in particular, as we have before remarked, breed in the friths and on our coasts, where the fry remain till they commence their migration to more distant regions. While, therefore, they continued floating up and down with the tide on the coasts, great quantities of them could not but be destroyed, together with the fry of other sea-fishes, and of the salmon in their descent from the rivers, in those yairs. A great herring fisher * has remarked many years ago :—

"In an arm of the sea where a shoal of herrings had been known to spawn the preceding winter, I have *seen* the fry moving towards the ocean during a considerable time in the early part of the summer. *They always keep near the shore*, and double every headland in their way, in order that they may not be driven out of their course by the tides and storms in the Channel. Perhaps there may be other causes why *they keep near the shore*, as that they may be out of the reach of larger fishes, and may have opportunities of picking up those small insects which swarm on the surface."

Now, observe what Mr John Steavenson states in the Committee :—

"I am acquainted with two or three yairs in the Moray Frith. I consider them most destructive. They are not only destructive of the fry of salmon, but destructive *of the fry of every other description of fish;* so much so, that it has come within my knowledge that *carts* have been loaded with *the fry of fishes*—I will not say of salmon, but of salmon among others—and sent to market."

And Mr Leslie, another witness in the Committee, states :—

"Both yairs and stake-nets are destructive of fry. I have *seen* five large basketfuls of fry taken out of a stake-net, and about a fifth part of them were salmon-fry. Yairs are *still more destructive*."

* Mr Melville.

Here, then, is full elucidation of the motives which induced the ancient Legislature to prohibit yairs and all such engines on the coasts, or in waters within reach of the *tide*, where, as stated by the witnesses, such quantities of the fry of sea fishes and of all fishes were destroyed by them, as expressed in the statutes. Let us then take a glance at these abused statutes, and see where the ambiguity so much complained of in the Scotch Court is to be found, or whether anything appears in them contrary to this plain common-sense construction of them. The first is the one already cited—the words of which we will repeat—viz. the Statute Rob. I. 1318 :—

" Omnes illi qui habent croas, vel piscarias, vel stagna, aut molendina, in aquis ubi ascendit mare et se retrahit, et ubi salmunculi, vel smolti, vel fria *alterius generis* piscium, *maris*, vel aquæ dulcis, ascendunt et descendunt," &c.

The words of this statute, then, correspond exactly with what has been stated by the witnesses. There is not one word in it which can show that the prohibition was intended to be restricted to *rivers*. The fry of *sea* fishes, and of all fishes, is conclusive on the subject ; for if the fry of sea-fishes are not to be found on the coasts of the sea, where are we to look for them ? And had not the Legislature the same power of legislation in all parts of the kingdom, at least within flood-mark? and on the sea-coasts as well as on those of friths, or on the banks of rivers ? If the power of the Legislature be not denied on the coasts of the sea, or that the fry of sea fish are to be found there, we defy any man to show that the prohibitions in the statutes do not extend to it.

In the discussions which took place regarding this statute, a manifest error was committed by the Court in translating the word *mare*, in the expression, " *In aquis ubi ascendit* mare *et se retrahit*," literally, in waters where the *sea* ebbs and flows, instead of where the *tide* ebbs and flows, which is the meaning of the expression. The reason why the tide is mentioned at all in the statutes, is because it is only where the tide ebbs and flows, as before remarked, that yairs could be placed. To prohibit them, therefore, in " waters where the *tide* ebbs and flows," was, in fact, a general prohibition, since nowhere else could they be erected. Now the operation of the tide cannot be expressed in the Latin language, except by the word mare: *fluxis et refluxis* MARIS. The words, "*In aquis ubi ascendit* mare *et se retrahit*," therefore, clearly mean in waters, generally, where the *tide* ebbs and flows;* and this is placed beyond doubt by the words which follow—viz. where the fry of any fish of the *sea*, or of fresh water, or of *any* kind of fish, can be destroyed. We believe that this obvious error of translating literally the word *mare* into sea instead of *tide*, tended greatly to mislead the Court in their construction of the statutes. In the literal sense of the word, the sea flows into very few of the Scotch *rivers*—indeed into none which fall into friths, as most of them do, where it is not the sea, but their own fresh or brackish water, that is driven back into them by the reflux of the tide; so that, in fact, the statutes, on *their* interpretation of them, would apply only to the few rivers which fall into the sea direct.

When the Kintore case was in the House of Lords, the Lord Chancellor, in alluding to this statute, upon which he laid great weight, as the model statute, remarked that the words "*ascendunt et descendunt*" appeared to him to denote the ascent and descent of the fry of salmon in *rivers;* and this seems to have been one of his lordship's reasons for affirming the judgment in that miserably mismanaged case, which has laid the foundation of interminable litigation all over Scotland. If his lordship had studied the nature of salmon, he would have known that the fry never *ascend* a river as fry; it would be contrary to their instincts. "As soon," says a salmon-fisher, "would a feather go against the wind as salmon-fry ascend a river." Descend they must, on their migration to the

* In Scotland the words where the sea ebbs and flows, and where the tide ebbs and flows, are deemed synonymous. The expression, "In waters where the tide ebbs and flows," was in fact the most general and comprehensive the Legislature could use; for it included, with the conciseness peculiar to the Scotch Acts, in one word all descriptions of water—whether fresh, salt, or mixed—in short, every part where the prohibited engines could be placed; and it would be absurd to suppose, that even if one Legislature erred, so many successive Parliaments would have used the same mode of expression, if it was not deemed the best suited to convey their intentions.

sea, but they never ascend except as grilses or salmon. The words alluded to by his lordship are therefore the strongest proof that it was *not* to rivers the clause alludes, since the fry of salmon, as we have said, *never* ascend rivers; the words mean merely the ascending and descending, or flowing up and down of the fry of all fishes on the shores, with the tide, by which they are carried into and destroyed in the yairs, which, if they remained stationary, could not happen. If a cart-load of fry were taken out of a yair in one tide, there might be another cart-load carried into it by the next tide,—the constant flowing up and down of the fry with the tide along the shores rendering them liable to destruction every tide in those engines, which shows the good sense with which the statutes were framed, prohibiting fixed engines in all waters to which the tide reached.

The next is the statute of James I., 1424, which ordains that

"All cruives and yairs set in *fresche* waters, where the sea filles and ebbes, the quhilk destroys the fry of all fishes, be destroyed and put away for ever mair notwithstanding ony privilege given to the contrair; and they that has cruives in *fresche* waters, that they gar keep the laws anent Saturday's slap, and that ilk heck of the cruives be three inches wide, as the auld statute requires," &c.

Any one who reads this statute must see at once that there is an *error* in the word *fresche* in the first part of the clause, which prohibits cruives in fresh waters, and then states that those who have cruives in "*fresche* waters" must regulate them according to law. The error is so palpable that any explanation seems almost unnecessary. If the word fresh be omitted in the first part of the clause, the statute will be quite consistent with the rest of the statutes; and this alone is sufficient to show that the word was an error, to whatever cause it was owing.—It will farther be evident,

First,—Because the clause prohibits cruives and yairs in fresche waters, where, it says, they destroy the fry of all fishes: but "the fry of all fishes" are never found in fresh waters: so that it is quite evident the word *fresche* could not have been in the original statute.

Second,—The word "fresche," in both parts of the clause, makes nonsense of the act. One of them *must* therefore have been an error, on this ground alone. The error could not have been in the latter part of the clause, because cruives are *allowed* in fresh waters in the whole of the acts. The error *must*, therefore, necessarily be in the insertion of the word in the first or prohibiting part of the clause ;—which is confirmed by the fact, that the word will not be found in that part in a single one of all the other statutes.

Third,—In a subsequent statute, wherein the words of this statute are expressly cited, the error does not appear—from which it may be presumed that, in the original statute, it did not, as we said, exist. The words of this statute are as follow :

" Act 1477.—Item, It is statute and ordained that the Act made of before be King James First anent cruives *set in waters,* be observed and keepit—the quhilk bears in effect that all cruives and yairs *set in waters where the sea fills and ebbs, destroys the fry of all fishes,* be put away and destroyed for evermore," &c.

The omission of the word, therefore, in this statute, which expressly cites the former, is, we conceive, sufficient proof that the error did not exist in the original statute—or, if it did, that it was deemed so palpably an error, that it was omitted in the next statute, and, indeed, in the *whole* of the subsequent statutes on record. There is not one of these reasons which is not sufficient, even singly, to show that the word was a mere error, wherever it originated. Remove the error, and the statute is in all other respects consistent with the other statutes. If the word was *not* an error, then the clause, as it stands, is, as we said, *nonsense,* and the statute should be passed over, there being no lack of statutes on the subject. But even if it were not nonsense, at the very worst all that could be said is, that it prohibits yairs in *fresh* waters, where yairs could not be placed ; but that is no reason why the subsequent statutes should not prohibit them in salt water, or on the coasts—that is, in those parts where they could be placed, and where they would destroy fry of all descriptions or *of all fishes.* It would, indeed, be extraordinary if this statute were to neutralise or defeat all the subsequent statutes.—We have heard of statutes repealing former statutes, but never before of one which annulled those which came *after* it. It is singular, that though the clause in this statute, owing to the error we have stated, is, as we have said, absolute nonsense, upon which it would be just as great nonsense to say that law can be founded, and upon which no court on earth, composed of men of common sense, would indeed attempt to found law, the Court of Session clung to this statute and founded upon it more than upon all the others—so congenial was it to practice, which can extract good Scotch law even out of nonsense itself.

Some have tried to explain the clause, by saying that the word fresh in the one part meant the lower part of the river, and in the other the higher; but this nowise mends the matter, for in no part of fresh water could yairs be erected, and in no parts of them are the fry of *sea* fishes, or of all fishes, to be found. The Act, with the word "fresche" in the prohibitory clause, will be nonsense in any way in which they can dispose of it—such thorough nonsense, that no set of men who know principles would waste their time, or allow their understandings to be so muddled with quibbles and sophisms as to attempt to extract law out of it, or who would be so insensible to the claims of justice as to dispose by it of the properties of individuals every day, in a course of litigation which they cannot but see must be *ruinous* to all involved in it.

It is needless to follow the statutes minutely any farther, the whole of them being of the same uniform import. The statute 1469 prohibits prynnes or narrow masses set in rivers that have their course to the sea, or set *within flood-mark of the sea*, meaning thereby, as stated in the Court of Session, the mouth of a *fresh-water* river.

The statute 1488 ordains that all yairs and fish-dams that are in *salt* water, where the sea (tide) ebbs and flows, be utterly destroyed, as well those that pertain to our Sovereign Lord, as all others throughout the realm; and that cruives set in *fresh* water be made according to law. It will be observed that, while the words of this Act furnish additional proof that the word "*fresche*" in the prohibitory clause of the Act 1424 was an *error*, as we have said,—they expressly show that it was in *salt* water, or on the coasts, that yairs were truly prohibited, as destructive of the fry of all fishes : yet *salt* water is interpreted into *fresh* water ; thus directly falsifying the statute.

The statute 1489 anent cruives and fish-yairs which destroy the fry of fishes and *hurt the common profit of the realm*, ordains that they be all utterly destroyed, and that the cruives in *fresh* waters be three inches wide. The words of this statute bear out what has been stated to have been the primary object of the Legislature—viz. an anxiety for the preservation of the fry of all fishes of every kind along the coasts ; but it was supposed that the destruction of cartloads of the fry of sea fishes in the yairs on the coasts was no *hurt to the common profit of the realm*, and, therefore, we were assured that the prohibition of yairs was intended only for the rivers. The very way, indeed, in which fresh waters are mentioned in the Acts—" *and they that have cruives in fresh waters* "—shows that it was to a different description of waters the prohibitions applied.

The statute 1563 ordains that all cruives and fish-dams which are in *salt* water that ebbs and flows—those in the water Solway alone excepted—be utterly destroyed, and that the cruives in *fresh* waters be made according to law. Nothing can be more correct than the mode of expression in this Act. It is free from all negligence in point of style, while it confirms the whole tenor and import of the former statutes, all having evidently the same object in view. If there was not another Act upon the Statute-Book, this Act alone should be quite sufficient for the purpose. The Legislatures by whom this and the other later Acts were framed, were undoubtedly better judges of the meaning of the former statutes, and of the intentions of former Legislatures, than some of the present day can pretend to be ; but let the intentions of those who framed the earlier statutes have been what they might, nobody will say that the subsequent Legislatures might not make *further* enactments if they thought fit ;—or, that even if the original statutes had limited the prohibition of yairs to fresh waters—which most assuredly was not the case—the subsequent Legislatures might not have extended the prohibitions to *salt* water, if they chose to do so ; and that they have done it—whether as a new enactment, or as a continuation of the old, it matters not—must be plain to all who read the Acts. While these later statutes, therefore, remain on the Statute-Book, the engines in question are beyond a doubt illegal in *salt* water, which comprehends the whole coasts of the kingdom—unless, indeed, the mere opinion of judges, as we said before, shall be deemed equivalent to an Act of Parliament, by which the statutes are repealed, or, which is the same, rendered useless.

All then, we repeat, that is necessary to understand these statutes is merely to read them, as all acts of the Legislature intended *for the guidance of the people* ought to be read, in the plain common-sense meaning of the words, when it is not possible that the intentions of the Legislatures by which they were framed can be mistaken. No series of statutes can be more consistent, nor more full of good sense and knowledge of the subject to which they relate. All the absurdity imputed to them is owing, not in the least to themselves, but to the ridiculous constructions which have been forced upon them.

Some weight has been given to the opinion of Lord Stair— who remarks,

"There is a special way of fishing by cruives and yairs, both in fresh water and salt, all which cruives are absolutely prohibited to be set in rivers in so far as the tide ebbs and flows, as being destructive of the fry of all fishes."*

Lord Stair's opinion is unquestionably entitled to respect in most cases; but on the point in question he admits that no cases had been tried, and seems to have bestowed but little attention upon it. The truth appears to be, that, when he wrote his book, he found it necessary to say something on the subject; and the little he did say, he said very superficially, probably from a mere cursory glance at the statutes, which, at the time, were deemed but of little importance, and which have scarcely ever been looked at by lawyers previous to the stake-net questions. Had his Lordship taken time to reflect, he would have seen the absurdity of supposing that the "*fry of all fishes*" could be destroyed in any part of rivers or fresh

*—B. 2, tit. 5.

waters. He can, therefore, be considered no authority in the matter. It was a subject out of his usual course of study, and which had probably never occupied his mind for half an hour. Had he been engaged in its investigation, like the learned judges of the present day, for the best part of a quarter of a century, the case would be very different. His Lordship was not infallible more than other mortals. He had no other means of forming an opinion but from the statutes themselves, and these statutes are now before us just as they were under his eyes, and are better authority than all the lawyers in the universe. If his Lordship's shade takes now and then a peep into the Parliament House, to see what is going on there, it must have been sadly grieved at the use that has been made of an inadvertent expression on a point which he had evidently not studied, in depriving many of their fishing properties.

That there are still yairs of the old description to be seen on the coasts in different parts of the kingdom, can only prove breaches of the law. Such violations of the law must have occurred frequently even under the vigilant eyes of the ancient Legislature, which was no doubt the cause of the repetition of their acts;—and it is the less to be marvelled at that they should happen since. We wonder, if a case of this kind, where it could be proved that one of these yairs on the coasts, destroyed nine cartloads, or a ton *of fry of all fishes* in a tide, were to be brought before the Court of Session, it would be maintained, in the face of the express words of the statutes, that it did not come within the prohibitions, because not placed in a fresh-water river? If violations of the law were to operate as exemptions from the law, or were to render the law nugatory, we know not what law would be in force in the remote parts of the kingdom. There is a law against tracing hares on the snow, yet we have seen it openly practised even by their little lordships, the sheriff-substitutes of northern counties. It is, therefore, no wonder if the fishing laws should be so, and millions of the *fry of all fishes* be destroyed, where, however much the public interest should suffer thereby, no individual would choose to involve himself in law proceedings to prevent it—in a country where no man can institute a plea, on the *clearest* grounds, without being entangled in the mazes of chicanery,—uncertain as to the result, but always sure, be that what it may, of being well *fleeced*—and, perhaps, as in the cases of Houston and Gilchrist, of having some hundreds of pounds of costs to pay to the trespassers.

The effects of the Kintore decision have been most disastrous to many of the Scotch salmon-fisheries. Had the decision in that case been the same as in the Tay case, it would have put an end, at once, to all litigation on the subject; but those decisions being contrary to each other, the one declaring stake-nets illegal in friths, the other legal in the sea, a door has been opened to endless litigation, there being no decided principle by which a line of distinction can be drawn, in waters varying so much from each other, to ascertain exactly where an engine is legal, or where it is not. In every case, all the defence necessary is just to assert that the engine complained of is situated in the *sea;* and should it be in water as fresh as if it were taken out of a fountain, it will answer all the ends of delay, chicanery, and injustice, and the most scandalous spoliation of property for at least three or four years: while the injured party, thus despoiled of his property, involved in all the chicanery of the Scotch complicated system, and ruined by expenses, has every chance, through the treachery of his agent, or some whim or crotchet of the Court, of being ultimately cast, in spite of the justice of his case, with costs. Such are the effects of our present blessed system. Since the decision on the Kintore case, so many bag-nets have been placed in the sea, up to the very mouths of the rivers Dee and Don, that only one-fourth of the fish usually caught in those rivers is now permitted to enter them, the other three-fourths being intercepted in those engines. Yet these rivers seem just as much entitled to legal protection as the Tay; and, assuredly, the statutes were never meant for partial operation, for nothing can be more general than the words in which they are expressed; extending, as has been shown, to all waters within reach of the *tide*, whether fresh, salt, or mixed. We trust the proprietors of the North and South Esks will bring a case from these rivers into Court, rather than be *for ever* exposed to such destructive engines. We think, that before the present able and enlightened judge, who presides in the Court of Appeal, they would have every chance of success, notwithstanding the decision in the Kintore case. In one of the stages of the Tay case, the eminent judge who then sat on the woolsack said, that "he was not prepared to say, *even if the case could not be distinguished from the former one*, it would not be carrying the matter a great deal too far to say that, *from what might be stated on the statutes*, a different view might not be taken in this case."*

We will even go further, and state our conviction, that if the Kintore case itself were brought again into the Court of Appeal, at the instance of an heritor who had not been a party in the former case, a different judgment would be obtained. The judgment of the Court of Session in that case, affirmed in the Court of Appeal, was founded upon a construction of the statutes not consistent with common sense, as has been already fully shown—viz. that "Waters where the tide flows and ebbs, and where the fry of any fish of the *sea*, or of fresh water, or the fry of all fishes, are destroyed," only meant rivers, or fresh waters, where the fry of *sea* fishes, or of all fishes, are never, and can never, be found;—and, further, that salt water means fresh water—and within flood-mark of the SEA only the lower part of a river—all of which is, on the very face of it, downright *absolute nonsense;* and as nonsense CANNOT be law, nor law be founded in nonsense,—particularly when the statutes are excellent sense in the natural construction of the words—it follows that the judgment cannot be held to be a valid one, nor in any degree influence that in any other case which may be brought forward.

* *March* 26, 1805.

SECTION VI.

RIVERS, FRITHS, ETC.

Le premier devoir d'un juge est d'être juste avant d'être formaliste. C'est un grand abus dans la jurisprudence que l'on prenne pour loi les rêveries et les erreurs d'hommes sans aveu qui donnent leurs sentimens pour des lois.
                                                            MONTESQUIEU.

IF the plain natural common-sense construction had been put upon the statutes, it would, as we have seen, have put an end at once to all stake-net questions, in all parts, and saved much trouble, as well as great destruction of individual property, and immense expense to the country in litigation; but it having been declared that the general word waters meant *rivers*—or fresh waters—where the prohibited engines could not be erected, and that salt water that ebbs and flows means exactly the *reverse*—it ought at least, in mercy to litigants, to have been told to the country what was understood to be *rivers*, and to what precise parts the statutes, in the construction given them, *do* apply. But we suspect this to be no easy matter: if we set out in error, every step subsequently taken has only involved proceedings deeper and deeper in absurdity. If it took *fourteen* years to discover that the word waters meant fresh-water rivers, which a single serious perusal of the statutes would have at once refuted, the sixteen years that have followed have not determined either what are to be considered as rivers, or where they are to terminate—points which continue still as much involved in darkness as ever—and which are subjects of constant and endless litigation and expense to all concerned in the fishery.

By the usage of Scotland, even at this day, and such assuredly was the usage at the periods when the statutes were made, a river is deemed just what is termed the river proper, or body of fresh water, contained within its own channel and banks, and before it falls within the shores or *local* boundaries of a frith or the sea—the only water in short, within reach of the tide, where yairs could *not* be erected—though the Court say it was there only the erection of such is forbid: the only water within reach of the tide where the fry of sea fishes or of all fishes are *not* to be found, though it is there only the Court say the destruction of them was prohibited—all which cannot be too often repeated, or be made too glaring. It is indeed singular, that absurdity is never considered a bar to a legal fiction, or argument, or nicety; being deemed just as good law as anything else, of which we could give instances without number. We have never heard that this is the case in other countries, even among the most uncivilised nations, all of whom appear to pay some regard to common sense. Had our lawyers, when conning over the statutes, said to themselves, These statutes describe the prohibited engines as *actually* destroying the fry of *sea* fishes, and of all fishes. Such fry are never found in rivers, and certainly they are not found there exclusively. This shows that the word "waters" was used in its general sense, and we have no right to *force* a construction upon it, which is contradicted by every other word in the statutes, and which, in fact, would make nonsense of them. But they do not accustom themselves to such reasoning. They do not take time for it, or bestow so much attention on the cases that come before them. Besides, if it be deemed proper to declare absolute nonsense to be law, who will dare to say otherwise? Is it the Scotch Press? It is cowed into the most abject submission. No country ever owed less to its Press than Scotland. Is it the Scotch Bar, composed of many men born with generous minds, but who, under practice, become heartless and sophisticated, and swim with the stream? We have often grieved to see a body for whom we entertain respect, have so little for themselves.

The Scotch Law has, in fact, ALTERED the statutes—that is, it has altered the import and plain meaning of the statutes, and substituted a novel law in their room, which is declared to be law. The statutes prohibit yairs in waters, generally, where the tide ebbs and flows—and the new law restricts this to rivers or fresh waters; the next point was, therefore, to define the rivers or parts to which this new law was to apply: but this has not been done, during even the quarter of a century which has elapsed since the new law was declared; so that the matter remains, as we have said, still involved as much in darkness and confusion as ever. We are told the prohibition of fixed engines is confined to rivers—to fresh waters; but what those rivers or fresh waters are, or whether they include the whole, or only a part, or what part, of friths or estuaries, we are still as ignorant of as the child unborn.

By the usage of Scotland, as we have remarked, rivers mean just what is termed the river proper, or body of fresh water contained within its own channel and banks, and before it falls within the shores or local boundaries of a frith or the sea. But the new lawgivers, though clinging still to the word *river*, which is never once mentioned in the prohibitory clause of the statutes, seem to be aware of the absurdity of restricting the prohibition to the rivers proper, and appear therefore disposed to extend them more or less into the friths, and to consider a part of the friths as fresh-water rivers, and the rest as the sea, —sweeping the useful denomination of Friths entirely from the map of the country, and dividing them between the Rivers and the Sea. The difficulty, however, was how to do so, or by what means, without the aid of the magical rod of Moses, to divide a frith, as he divided the Red Sea, into two parts, the one to be considered a *fresh*-water river, the other the pure unadulterated salt *sea?* This was a point quite sufficient to exercise wisdom, if wisdom could condescend to bestow a thought upon the matter. The lawgivers were undoubtedly sadly puzzled to extricate themselves out of this dilemma, into which their absurd construction of the statutes had led them, and which they could discover no principle to support. If, however, they could not make the division *de facto*, they did it in idea, and made the application *de facto*. How a rustic, or other unsophisticated son of nature, would stare, if he were gravely told that his mountain stream, which discharged itself into a lake, did not end with its channel or banks, but extended half way into the lake—or in other words, that half the lake was the mountain stream, and the other half a quite different water: he might, perhaps, admire such exalted notions, as he would the reveries and *tourbillons* of Descartes—or he might, perhaps, take to his heels, thinking he was in unsafe company; but as to the actual possibility of the thing, it would never once enter into his head, or we believe into any heads save those of learned men, so brimful of legal lore, and so mystified with legal niceties and subtleties, as to be unable to distinguish sense from nonsense.

It is true friths differ from lakes in the quality of the water, but that nowise mends the matter. Friths are, in fact, bodies of *mixed* water, composed of the fresh water of the rivers flowing in at the one extremity, and of sea water flowing in with the tide at the other,—both blended together by such imperceptible degrees, by the constant action of the tide, that all the chemical knowledge of a Sir H. Davy would be unable to draw a line of distinction between them, or to say at what *precise* part all above could be called a river or fresh water, and all below the *sea*. Besides, even were it practicable to fix upon such a line, which it evidently is not, it would vary with every flood in the rivers, so that what would be declared to be the sea in the morning, might be the river in the afternoon.

It is, therefore, clear, that if we admit any parts of a frith to be a river, in the extended sense of the word as used by other nations, though not in the Scotch sense, they must include the *whole* of the frith to the *fauces terræ*, since no INTERMEDIATE line of distinction can be drawn. In truth, the *fauces terræ*, or local boundaries, are the natural boundaries of all waters. It may be the *same* water which flows out of a river into a millrace, or into a canal; it is the locality alone that makes the difference. An eminent quibbler in the Tay Case, which, as we have said, was a mere mass of quibbles from one end to the other, argued that "the frith being, he said, the sea, it would be unmeaning tautology to maintain that the sea flowed into itself." He might have added, that a river, which flows out of a lake, being the same water, it would be nonsense to say that the river is not the lake. Salt water *from* the sea flows with the tide into all the great rivers in the world; but no man ever thought of calling those rivers the *sea* on that account. That was an absurdity reserved for the Scotch Law. When water flows from one body within the *local* or natural boundaries of another body of water, it becomes, necessarily, a part thereof. If salt water alone, without extent, constituted the sea, a horse-pond might be filled with it, and be called the sea. But friths, as before remarked are bodies *per se*, composed of *mixed* water, which are neither fresh-water rivers on the one hand, or the sea on the other; though in the Tay Case they were sometimes called the one, and sometimes the other; and sometimes both, just as it suited parties to state.

In that celebrated Case, the Court being greatly puzzled where to draw a line of demarcation between the river and the sea, across the frith, in order to divide the waters above from the waters below; and not knowing how to act, in the dilemma into which they had brought themselves, a scientific gentleman who had been philosophising and taking levels in the estuary, appeared upon the scene, and stated to the Court, that the proper criterion for fixing the termination of all rivers was the *tide*, that is, that a river terminates, not with its banks, or with the *fauces terræ* of the frith—but exactly in that precise part, WITHIN THE FRITH, where the medium tide is always either ebbing or flowing. Here, then, was a principle just such as the Court wanted, for dividing a frith into two parts, without the aid of the magical rod of Moses, and for showing the termination of one body of water *within* another, by a power which acts upon both indiscriminately. The principle having the merit of novelty, and above all of *science*, was hailed in the Parliament House with universal applause. It was grand, and was not adopted, only because it was supposed to have been unknown to the mere common-sense legislators by whom the statutes were framed. It is quite obvious that the tide must flow up all rivers, more or less, just according to the DEPTH of their channels and the levelness of the ground. It flows up the Thames to Richmond—and we believe the medium low-water mark is somewhere about Putney; so that, according to the above criterion, all below Putney, which is higher up than all the London bridges, is the SEA; and only all above it the river Thames. We know not what the Thames watermen would say to this; or how it would affect the Lord Mayor's jurisdiction in the river, which we suppose would not extend into that part of it at London, converted by our civil engineer into the *sea*. In the river Potomack, again, the tide flows above Washington, a distance of upwards of 280 miles. We wonder how much of this internal space would, by the same criterion be termed the river, and how much the SEA. Honest Jonathan would be quite delighted to learn that he possessed so many inland seas which he never dreamt of. But the Court rejected it, and had to hunt out for another principle for themselves, and at length hit upon one not a whit better—viz. the charters or titles of parties—as if charters or legal documents could be proof of a *natural fact*. They accordingly extended the river to Drumly Sands, but without prejudice, they added, to those who had *sea*-fishings above that point, that is in the *river*, which is downright nonsense, and thus ended that very drumly Case, just as it had begun—to the great edification of all concerned.

In another case, of recent date, from the Frith of Dornoch, relative to a fixed engine placed in the very channel of the water, in that part not so broad at low water as the Thames at London Bridge, and which, though the water was quite fresh, the party, as a last desperate resource, chose to affirm was the *sea*, knowing that in the Scotch Court it would ensure him three years *mala fide* possession, till the point was determined, a remit was made to another civil engineer, who was directed by the Court to report his opinion whether the part in question was the sea or not, as if the mere *opinion* of this man were sufficient to authorise the disposal of the vested rights of individuals. Our engineer accordingly inspected the part; he reported to the Court, that as they had been greatly *puzzled*, and the vested rights of parties greatly distracted, by the various denominations of friths, *fiords*, rivers, and estuaries, he would supply them with a criterion that would settle all matters at once, being applicable to all cases. He adopted the former

principle of the *level* of the tide, only rendering it more ridiculous by applying it to the *bottom* instead of the surface of the water (perhaps on the ground that truth lies at the bottom of the well), in order, as he expresses it, " to ascertain the point at which the level of the sea touches the land *under the superstratum of fresh or drainage water ;* " and, upon this principle, which he assures the Court proved quite satisfactory in the Thames and the Dee, in proving both rivers to be the SEA, he declares the part in question, where he admits the water to be quite *fresh* above, and only brackish at the bottom, to be the SEA !*
Having settled this point so satisfactorily, and in a way so consonant with science, if not with common sense, he next tells the Court that he has farther discovered, that " the waters of the frith obey the same general law which regulates the ocean, being thereby affected in their flux and reflux ;" in other words, that the tide ebbs and flows there just as it does elsewhere.

We were anxious to see how these great discoveries, which were to remove the *puzzles* of the judges and settle the distracted rights of parties in all time coming, would be received by the Court—and no doubt the discoverer was just as anxious himself to witness his triumph, and to receive the compliments of the Court on the occasion. Unfortunately the matter came before an Ordinary, *qui en savait plus que lui*—the Lord Moncreiff, whose superior mind saw through the whole juggle at once—and who treated the superstratum of *drainage* water and the *fresh*-water sea with utter contempt ; but it was paid for. It is a common practice with the Court of Session to make remits of this kind to men, whose reports, not being made on *oath*, can be of no value, or have any other effect than to increase expense upon litigants. We have seen many such remits to land-surveyors, agriculturists, and dabblers in science, but we have never seen one where the business was not, to all appearance, jobbed.

In the Cromarty Frith stake-nets are still in their full glory, and the rivers nearly useless. In the river Alness, which discharges itself into that frith, and where, of yore, dozens of salmon might be angled in a forenoon, scarcely a fish is now to

* This is exactly the case in the Thames at Woolwich.

be seen. The water of this frith is some shades salter than in the adjacent friths, and this circumstance is deemed legally sufficient, it is alleged, to deprive the rivers in this estuary of the protection of the statutes, as if the *quality* of the water could defeat the claims of *justice*, or remove all protection from property. If the *fauces terræ* are the natural boundaries of friths, as of rivers, there is no frith in Scotland better defined than the frith of Cromarty: but it is said the *bay* is so fine, and the *anchorage* so good, that the whole British Navy might ride there with safety—and this was brought forward as an invincible, and, we believe, a successful argument, to show that it was not a water where the tide ebbed and flowed, or where fry of any kind could be destroyed, in the words of the statutes. The argument was doubtless quite unanswerable. But any argument, whether in point or not, will serve the purpose, where delay is wanted; and the worse the argument, in general the more effectual it seems to be in law.

In the Inverness Frith a stake-net has been condemned by the Court as illegal, at Redcastle, within a few miles of the river Beauly; while another stake-net at Culloden, still nearer to the river Ness, and therefore, according to the ideas of the Court with regard to the statutes, still more illegal, has been found to be directly the *reverse*, and has continued regularly at work, intercepting the fish of both rivers. In short, no man can know where an engine is illegal, or where it is not. No man can call his fishing property his own—or be sure, for one hour, that a fixed engine may not be run out immediately in front of it, and extinguish it at a stroke. Such is the state of the salmon-fishery at present; and if the sufferers look for redress—the redress of the dice-box—it is the merest chance that it will be even ultimately obtained, after *years* of litigation, while the expense, quite ruinous, is certain. In a case now under the consideration of the Court from the same frith, an issue has been sent to a jury to try, whether an engine, placed about midway between the illegal stake-net at Redcastle and the legal one at Culloden, is in a *river* or in the *sea?* The engine is in *mixed* water—between the river Beauly and the river Ness, and at many miles distance from the sea. It is therefore obviously neither in a river, nor in the sea, but in the mixed water of the frith, composed of both river and sea water; yet no alternative is left to the jury but to find, upon their *oath*, that it is in the one or the other. This is placing the jury in a pretty predicament. The Court might just as well force them to declare, upon their great oath, whether a mule was a horse or an ass! It is an excellent specimen of the manner in which matters are conducted. If the jury system is to be introduced into Scotland in all cases, in the simple way it is practised in England, and it would be an infinitely greater boon to the country than the Catholic Act was to Ireland, the Legislature in sending down the Act should send some English judges along with it, to infuse a little common sense into the proceedings, and prevent juries being forced to find, upon their oaths, that mules are either horses or asses, instead of being a compound of both.

It is needless to cite further instances of the practice in the Court, it being quite clear that the salmon-fishery must continue in its present anomalous state, until a return is made to a proper construction of the statutes. The sooner, then, the better—for until that be done, robbery, and spoliation of property, and injustice, and a constant waste of expense in litigation, must continue to take place. We would, therefore, recommend to the Court to adopt at once the TRUE common-sense construction of the statutes. All mortals are, doubtless, liable to err. It is the lot of that proud two-legged animal called Man; but it is only the self-important vulgar soul that persists in its errors: generous minds are ever ready, even impatient, to acknowledge and repair the evils which may have arisen from those they have unconsciously committed. If interdicts were granted in every instance against new engines, it would prevent much injustice taking place, and save the rights of many an injured individual: but these the Courts almost uniformly refuse to grant. They do not consider that, in suppressing a fixed engine, its owner loses in fact *nothing* which he possessed before; while every hour it is allowed to stand deprives the owner of some river or other of a portion of his property—of property that has been purchased, like all other property, on the faith of legal protection, and to which his right is as unquestionable as that of the stake-net proprietors, or coast heritors, is to their lands. On the score of *justice*, a doubt cannot exist on the subject; and, when real honest substantial justice is allowed to be constantly defeated by pretended fictions or sophisms of law, there is, assuredly, a radical fault *somewhere*—either in the constitution of the Court, or of the Judges.*

* The best Judges Scotland ever had were the English Judges sent down by Oliver Cromwell. Their administration of justice gave universal satisfaction, and their removal at the Restoration was as universally regretted. When their upright administration of the law was mentioned to Sir Hew Dalrymple, President of the Court of Session, he observed, "The deil thank them for a parcel of kinless chiels."

SECTION VII.

MR KENNEDY'S COMMITTEE.

> All that glisters is not gold.
> SHAKESPEARE.
>
> " Le monde est plein de fous,
> Et qui veut n'en voir,
> Doit se nicher dans un trou,
> Et casser son miroir."
> *French Author.*

THE proceedings of this Committee have made a considerable impression upon the public mind. To call these proceedings *evidence* would be ridiculous. They convey merely the opinions of the witnesses on a subject in which the personal interest of the whole of them was more or less concerned. Disinterested investigation in the leader of the Committee, or impartial statements on the part of the witnesses, we hold, therefore, to be entirely out of the question. Some of the witnesses, though not upon oath, spoke truth; others stated mere fictions and absurdities, to promote their own views;— the whole together forming such a mass of contradiction, that any man, personally unacquainted with the nature of the salmon-fishery, must rise from a perusal of it quite at a loss what to think of the matter. To show the spirit in which the business was carried, we shall cite what was afterwards stated in the Committee on the Bill by Mr Sheppard, an Irish gentleman, who had been sent over by the proprietors of the rivers in Ireland, and who had been previously examined in Mr Kennedy's Committee. The Committee ask him,—

"When you were examined before, your evidence was confined to the river Lee principally?"—"I was examined, I beg to say, with great respect to the Committee, only on ONE side of the question."

"On which side of the question?"—"I trust I am not indecorous in saying that there were no questions *asked me* that bore on the interest of the proprietors."

"You consider you were examined against the proprietors?"—"*I was asked such questions as bore against them.*"

Such was not the case with regard to the stake-net fishers, Johnstone, Halliday, Little, and Co., who were brought out in high style,—to show off their system to the best possible advantage, by statements sometimes so perfectly absurd as to be absolutely ludicrous. The Committee ask Johnstone,

"Is the Committee to understand that there are salmon which frequent the friths, and go out again to sea, without going up the river?"—"YES."

Now, we would like to ask Mr Kennedy how he conceived it to be *possible* for the witness to know whether there were or not? After the salmon *reach* our coast, and particularly after they enter the estuaries and rivers, it is their nature to conceal themselves as much as possible. No fisherman can trace their motions in a river or in a frith for five seconds together. He may see one leap out of the water occasionally, perhaps once or twice in a day, perhaps not once in a week, which is all he can know on the subject. He may see a salmon leap with his head downward with the ebb tide, if the rivers are in a low state; and he may see one, half an hour thereafter, leap with his head upward, returning with the flood-tide; but he cannot know whether it be the *same* fish or not, it being utterly beyond human power, as we said, to trace their motions *under water* for five seconds together; and yet Johnstone and Halliday, and other stake-net fishers, talk of both the motions and *intentions* of the fish, as they would of a flock of sheep upon a meadow.

The Committee, in the same strain, ask Mr Halliday,

"Are there a great many salmon which come into friths that do not go to the rivers, but return again to the sea?"—"There are a great many."

"Do you mean that they are going down *from their own natural impulse*, or from being carried down with the tide ?"—"They are going down from their own natural impulse with the tide."

"You mean to say that these fish are seeking to get to the sea ?"—"Yes, seeking down to get to the sea."

"You have no doubt that such is the fact ?"—"I am *certain* it is the fact."

Had Mr Kennedy known anything of the principles of the migratory system, he could never have supposed that, after the salmon had left their migratory abode in the ocean, and reached the mouths of the rivers, they would, without any apparent cause, turn back again, any more than a flock of lapwings or woodcocks would do so after having reached our shores, and would not have asked an ignorant man such ridiculous questions; which, besides, common sense might have showed him it was *impossible* the witness could know or answer; for what means could the witness, or any man, have of discovering whether the fish went down from *their own natural impulse*, with the tide; or, in short, whether they went down at all, since he could not see their movements under water even in the space of a hundred yards, much less over the whole expanse of the frith? And if the witness had been a sensible man, he would have answered,—"Sir, how do you suppose that I could trace the motions of the salmon that enter a frith, or know their intentions? we sometimes find them in the ebb-traps of our engines, but farther than that I cannot say; if you want to know more, you must ask a seal, or some other marine animal, who sees what passes under water, and who alone can tell you." Mr Kennedy, however, continues,

"You do not consider that all the fish that are caught by stake-nets placed at the *mouth* of an estuary or river, are fish which would have gone into the river ?"—"No."

As if it were *possible*, as we have just said, for the witness to know anything about the matter. The Committee afterwards ask the witness,

"What do you conceive to be the *object* which *induces* salmon to visit the rivers at the early periods of the season ?"

Mr Kennedy might have as well asked him what he conceived to be the *object* which *induces* the cuckoo to visit this country? The one question would be just as sensible as the other. The witness, however, never at a loss for a reason, answers,

"One *evident* object is to get clear of the vermin called the sea-louse—and they come in search of *food* also. I consider a salmon to be in search of food wherever he goes."

If salmon come to rivers in search of food, they come to parts where there is very little food for them. Here we find the true haddock hypothesis—the fish swimming about in search of FOOD—for as to the system of migration, the witness never dreamt of such a thing, and as to the sea-lice, we have said enough already. The fresh water kills these lice, because any truly sea animal cannot exist in fresh water. We wonder Mr Halliday did not ask himself why all the salmon in the sea that are infected with these lice do not take the rivers *at once?* And how it happens that the salmon of *late* rivers have never those lice, like the salmon of the early rivers, in winter and spring, so as to "induce" them to enter the rivers *then?* Do the lice fix themselves regularly to the salmon of the early rivers in the early months, and to those of the late rivers in the late months? In short, as all the salmon got in stake-nets have lice upon them as well as the others, why do these salmon not also betake themselves to the fresh water as well as the rest? But it is useless to waste time in exposing such manifest absurdities.

It is amusing to see how minutely Mr Kennedy, whom Mr Sheppard accuses of asking him no questions that bore on the interest of river proprietors, brings out everything he conceives calculated to strengthen the stake-net system. He asks the above witnesses,

"Do the stake-net fishermen become expert sailors?"—"They do —a great many of them have gone into the sea service. There are several of them in the *ferries.* They become very much qualified to manage boats and small vessels along the coasts, and many of them arrive to be *captains of smacks* and coasters, and some of them have gone on board the *navy.*"

"Have they any other employment during close-time connected

with the fisheries?"—" Some of them have, but the greater part are tradespeople and labourers, principally *weavers.*"

Now, all the operations connected with stake-nets are carried on on dry ground. The stakes are planted—the nets are attached to them—and the fish are taken out of them at ebb-tide. Of all fishers, of whatever description, the stake-net fisher has the least connection with boats or with the water. Even his fish he carries to the ice-house on land, or to the vessel in harbour, that is to convey them to London; yet it is by these dry-shod *weavers,* rendered by stake-nets such expert seamen, that our navy is to be manned.—*Certes,* the country is much indebted to Mr Kennedy for bringing so important a fact into notice.

The Reverend Dr Fleming is a witness of a higher caste. He is a naturalist, and a man of science;—he has written an article, he says, on Ichthyology in the Encyclopædia;—and he knows more, his friends the stake-net owners tell us, regarding the natural history of salmon than all the men in his Majesty's dominions. We must, therefore, bestow a little more notice upon him. Johnstone and Halliday have stated, as we have seen, that salmon are induced to enter rivers to get rid of sea-lice, and in search of food.—The Doctor has discovered another reason, viz.—terror! He says,

" Towards the *heads* of estuaries salmon must be frequently induced to enter rivers properly so called, in order to escape from the numerous foes which persecute them in the estuaries."

" How far (the Committee ask) do you think the salmon may go into a river when not obstructed, and return to the sea without having spawned?"—" A good deal must depend on the *degree* of terror of the fish,—its strength,—and the state of the river."

This is a *new* reason why salmon enter rivers, which certainly has no connection with any of what appear to be the principles of the migratory system. The degree of terror in the Tay fish must be very great, for many of them never stop till they reach Loch Tay.

We wonder how many *degrees* of terror salmon experience, or how long they continue. We always thought that the eye was the principal organ of terror in a salmon, and that in this point the adage, " Out of sight, out of mind," might be applied to him ; but the Doctor makes the length of his residence in a river to depend upon the strength of his MEMORY. What excellent memories salmon must therefore have ; for Mr Stephen has furnished proof that, after they enter rivers, they never leave them till they have spawned. We do not know if the Doctor is a phrenologist. Perhaps he has paid particular attention to the bump that denotes memory upon the nobs of the salmon, for we cannot conceive by what other means he could have made the discovery. We know not what foes persecute them at the *heads* of friths. Now and then a solitary seal appears there, but their principal foes in those parts are the fishermen. In another part the Doctor has told us that salmon enter rivers in the early part of the season from a " premature exercise of their instincts." Perhaps there are no foes, at that time, at the heads of the friths to drive them into the rivers, or the one cause may have produced the other—the terror occasioning the *premature* exercise of the instinctive functions. Medical men say that terror frequently produces premature or abortive effects. It seems to be when the rivers are in flood that the foes of the salmon, from the seals to the sea-lice, are busiest, for they then drive them into the rivers without ceasing. Which of all these reasons—viz. the premature exercise of their instinctive functions, the quality of the water, sea-lice, or terror, is the *true* cause of the salmon entering the rivers, naturalists only can determine, but we think the whole may be justly termed the Hodge-Podge System.

The Doctor continues :—

" When a fish has advanced a considerable distance into the freshwater stream, *instigated by its own natural instincts*, I should be inclined to think it would proceed to the place of its destination without again returning till it had *spawned*."

The Doctor first tells us that the length a salmon will go into a river depends upon the *degree* of terror he experiences :—and then he informs us, that after he has got a considerable way into it, " INSTIGATED BY HIS OWN NATURAL INSTINCTS," he proceeds to the place of his DESTINATION. But why should he suppose that, after salmon had entered a river at all, they would return before they had reached the place of their *destination?* Does he think their " natural instincts" do not begin to operate till they advance a " considerable distance" into the river? At *what* distance do their instincts commence to operate? How DID HE ASCERTAIN THE FACT, or that, after entering a river, they do return to the sea? Has he made any experiments to that effect? Did he tie a bladder to a salmon that had entered the Tay, in order to trace his motions under water? If he had done this, we believe the salmon would have soon led him up the river, *au pas de charge,* through briars and thorns, till he saw his balloon fairly skimming the surface of Loch Tay ;

> Monsieur l'Abbé où allez vous?
> Vous allez vous casser le cou,
> Vous allez sans chandelle, &c.
> *French Song.*

We have heard of a person who tied a goose to a salmon that was caught a short way within a river, and returned into it; but, though the salmon often drew the goose under water, he never attempted to return to the sea. That would be contrary to his instincts. Probably it was some experiment of this sort that enabled Johnstone and Halliday to trace the course of the fish returning from the rivers through the expanse of the estuaries. If a goose was tied to each salmon, what a glorious fleet of geese would be seen sailing down the friths, cackling, into the repositories of the stake-net fishers, who, perched upon their engines, and waving their hats with exultation, would welcome their friends into port.

The idea that salmon, after having reached their river, return again to the sea, before they have accomplished the objects nature had in view in bringing them there, is equally inconsistent with the principles of the migratory system as with common sense. When the migratory tribes of birds reach their destination, they immediately disperse. In like manner, when the salmon reach their rivers, the *gregarious* instinct which kept them together in the sea being no longer necessary, having performed its functions, *ceases,* and the fish disperse all over the river. Their migratory voyage is then at an end. This may show the absurdity of supposing that salmon are constantly running down from the rivers to the sea—for which there is not a particle of proof.

The worthy Doctor calls the salmon a *sea* fish, because he resides, during his migration, in the sea. On the same principle, he might call a Highland stot, bred in Skye and fed in Yorkshire, an English bullock. He, however, again admits, as we shall see immediately, that salmon *belong* to the rivers; and if they belong to the rivers, how can they belong to the sea, or be sea fishes?

The Committee ask him,—

"Do you believe that the fish always return to the same rivers?" —"Generally speaking," says he, "they may, perhaps, *endeavour* to return; but there are many circumstances to derange their course, so as in fact to render it *impossible* that they should return to the river."

"But if they live, they are most likely to return to the river in which they were bred?"—"*Yes;* if they live, and are not deranged in their movements—conditions not likely ever to occur."

But why, Doctor, should they *endeavour* to return to the rivers in which they were bred, unless an instinct has been implanted in them for that purpose? Your admission of the endeavour implies an admission of the instinct; and yet you, a naturalist, can suppose that the instinct is inadequate for the purpose for which it was intended; which, in other words, is to deny the principle of perfection in the works of the Deity. This we would not expect from a son of the church. Being further pushed on the point by the Committee, the Doctor continues,—

"The fish, after they have left the river, seem to retire to *the remoter parts of the ocean*—indeed, to parts with which we are wholly unacquainted; but we are in some measure acquainted with the number of foes which unceasingly persecute them, and which must necessarily mix the families, or *tribes*, BELONGING to the different estuaries, and to the different *rivers* connected with those estuaries, and as salmon are obviously *gregarious* animals, it seems difficult to conceive how, after such intermixture and persecution, the different BREEDS of fish, of the DIFFERENT RIVERS, could again separate from the common flock, to collect into original groups.

Here, then, is a direct admission of all that we have been maintaining. The different BREEDS *belonging* to the DIFFERENT RIVERS is fairly acknowledged; and it is for the Doctor to show how there could be different breeds with promiscuous intermixture, or if the fish did not keep separately in the sea, and return to their respective rivers. If this was not the case, no river could have a different breed, for all the breeds would be mixed. The breed that would be in one river one year, might be in another river, mixed with other breeds, the next. The Doctor's argument is, therefore, at perfect variance with itself. It is, in fact, nonsense. Does he suppose, too, that Omniscience, when he created grampusses and seals and salmon, did not *foresee* the effects that would result from such persecution, as he calls it—a persecution that is common to all the animal race, on land and in water—and so regulate the instincts of the salmon as to prevent the effects which the Doctor conceives must arise from it? The *fact* that the salmon DO return to their own rivers, and that each river STILL continues to possess its own peculiar variety of the species, shows that he is mistaken.

The Committee ask the Doctor,—

"Do you think that the fish of a particular river can be distinguished from the fish of other rivers?"—"I have heard experienced fishermen make the assertion, and I have heard other experienced fishermen give a flat contradiction to such a statement—so I have much hesitation in admitting that they are readily distinguished."

If there are, as the Doctor has said, different *breeds* belonging to different rivers, how does he suppose there can be different breeds, if they cannot be distinguished from each other? Can there be a difference without a distinction? If the different breeds cannot be distinguished, is it not nonsense to say there are different breeds? Whatever ignorant fishermen might have said, the Doctor should not advance an inconsistency. When so logical a head admits a *fact*, it should not deny the conclusion that *must* necessarily result from it.

The Committee farther ask,—

"Is it not a *fact* that salmon differ very much in form?"—"It certainly is a fact that salmon do differ *very considerably* in point of form from one another, as I have repeatedly witnessed by looking at the fish taken at the same place, and collected together in a boat."

"How do you account for individuals of the same species differing in form?"—" Precisely as individual differences are accounted for in other species of animals. Salmon are exposed, in their young state, to very different circumstances. Some are longer in the river after having left their spawning-beds than others—and it may be supposed, likewise, that during their residence in the sea they may have access to different quantities and different qualities of food. In fact, the ordinary circumstances that produce varieties in other individuals of other species, I should think likely to exist and produce individual differences in the salmon."

Having admitted that there are different BREEDS belonging to different rivers, we should think that it would be more consonant with the Doctor's sagacity, and to common sense, to impute the difference of form to that circumstance. If he saw salmon of different shapes collected in a boat in the Tay, he might have concluded that they were the fish of the Earne and of the Tay itself, and its different branches or tributary streams, which we suppose was the fact; but to impute difference of form to difference of feeding, was, of all reasons, the most absurd. Difference of feeding may increase the size or improve the condition of an animal; but how can it alter its form or shape? How could it make the whole of the salmon of one river, uniformly, and year after year, round or hog-backed, and others straight-backed? Would difference of feeding give a dray-horse the symmetry of a race-horse, or a mastiff the shape of a greyhound? We would recommend to the Doctor to keep this in view when he writes his next book on natural history.

The Committee ask the Doctor why he considers the grilse to be the young salmon, and not a distinct variety of the species? and he answers, with his usual tone of science,—

"Fish are known to breed long before they arrive at maturity; and as a *proof* that they do, it may be stated, that at the end of the season the salmon caught in a state fit for spawning are by no means of the same size; if, then, we are to take size as an *index of age*, we must arrive at the conclusion that salmon spawn at different ages, and before they have reached their full size."

We have all along thought that the Doctor's knowledge of

salmon was merely theoretical, picked up in his closet and from his conversations with his stake-net neighbours, and this answer to the question of the Committee is quite enough of itself to convince all the world of it. Who, that knows anything of the salmon fishery, would consider *size* an index of age, except with regard to fish of the same river ?—since the salmon of one river will be larger in one year than the salmon of another river will in ten. "A salmon of the Bush," says Mr Little, "will never grow to the size of a Shannon fish, were he to live to any age." In the same way, a young greyhound will grow larger in one year than a terrier would in twenty, were he to live so long, let the quantity or quality of his food, which the Doctor supposes alone make a difference in animals, be what it may.

The Doctor's ideas of spawning seem to be singular enough. He thinks that in this respect the Tay should be taken as a standard for all rivers :—

"I take the Tay," says he, "as a standard, because it is freed from anomalies—being the river which pours the greatest quantity of fresh water into the ocean, and it being the river which has produced the greatest quantity of salmon."

This is undoubtedly a very original idea—viz., of having a *standard* river, to regulate the spawning in other rivers. We only fear it will be somewhat difficult to make the salmon of all the rivers understand the necessity of regulating their breeding organs thereby ;—though perhaps the united wisdom of the Doctor, Mr Home Drummond, and Mr Kennedy, may contrive, with the aid of an Act of Parliament and new stake-net or other ingenious machinery, some means of effecting it, and of altering the natural constitution of the salmon race.

The Committee farther ask the Doctor, "whether an obvious diminution must not take place in those rivers where there are stake-nets in the estuaries?" Here the interest of the Doctor's dear stake-net friends was brought directly to the point, and he accordingly replies :—

"If stake-nets catch salmon advancing directly to the rivers, they *must* occasion a *corresponding* diminution in the river fisheries ; but such fish are *not* caught in stake-nets."

Upon what grounds could the Doctor take upon himself to assert that the salmon taken in stake-nets were *not* advancing to the rivers? What facts can he adduce in support of his opinion? We defy him to produce one single *fact* from which such a conclusion can be drawn. He has admitted that the salmon retire to *remote* parts of the ocean: what, then, does he suppose to be the object of their return but to reach the rivers? And does he, a naturalist, say that, when a shoal of these salmon enter an estuary, they are not all actuated by the same instincts? —Can he believe, without any *proof*, that different and contrary instincts exist in the same race—or the same tribe or family of animals? for he has admitted that the salmon-shoals are composed of the tribes or families belonging to the different rivers; and yet he thinks that the instinct of proceeding to the rivers, after having come from such a distance, was only implanted into some individuals of the shoal, and not into all. If salmon proceeded to or were caught in the rivers only at the spawning season, the Doctor would have some reason for the assertion; but he knows perfectly well that they are constantly going to the rivers, and that from the beginning of the season they are regularly taken there by the river fishers; and, therefore, to divide the shoals into fish that would go to the rivers, and fish that would not, or fish with and without instincts, or under the influence of contrary instincts, is an evident absurdity. In proceeding up the estuaries the fish do not go in a direct line to the rivers; they are sometimes in the channel, and sometimes not, according to the state of the tide. At low water they must be in the channel, as the sides of the estuaries are then dry, from the ebb of the tide; but at flood-tide they proceed in all parts of the estuaries, and it is then they are intercepted by stake-nets. The Doctor says that 30,000 were caught annually in the stake-nets of the Tay. These 30,000, therefore, in his opinion, came from the ocean, without the instinct of proceeding to the rivers being implanted in a single one of them, though all were equally charged with *spawn* as those which proceeded to the rivers, for he says that not one of them would be caught at the rivers. Why, we again ask, does he suppose these 30,000 left their migratory abode in the *remote* parts of the ocean to which he has told us he believes they retire? Why did they come upon our coasts at all, if they had no intention, or were impelled by no instinct, to proceed to the rivers? He ought to show us what their object was. It is evident that the Doctor fell into the stake-net error of considering salmon as mere common fishes like haddocks, swimming about the shores at random, and entering rivers as chance might direct, for the purpose of breeding; but then, how can he reconcile this belief that they migrate to REMOTE parts of the ocean, and his admission that they consist of tribes, or different breeds, or families *belonging* to the different rivers? In point of consistency, our naturalist is nowise better than the herd of stake-net fishers.

The Doctor further states that the capture of these 30,000 salmon by the stake-nets, occasioned neither a decrease of the price of salmon at market, nor a diminution of the produce of the river fisheries. It is not easy to reconcile these two facts. It is well known that the price of all articles at market depends upon the increased or diminished supply. A very little reflection upon the subject might have satisfied the Doctor, that there could not have been a *real* increase of so great a quantity as 30,000 fish, or it *must* have occasioned a fall in the market-price; and he ought, therefore, as we said before, to have hesitated before he threw the weight of his testimony, as a naturalist, into the scale of the stake-net fishers, particularly as the vicinity of his residence to Perth gave him ample means of ascertaining the truth. Had he been disposed to do this, Mr Buist could have shown him, as he showed the Committee, that the river fisheries fell off exactly in proportion to the increase of the stake-nets, till at length they scarcely produced a third of their usual quantity of fish, the other two-thirds being intercepted by those engines; and he could have ascertained the accuracy of the fact by a personal inspection of the books of the Dundee Shipping Company, by whose vessels the fish of both parties were sent to market. We have therefore nothing complimentary to say in favour of the Doctor's candour, any more than of his knowledge of the salmon-fishery. The stake-nets were no doubt, as we said before, very convenient in the vicinity of the Manse; but *justice* had also had some claims on our naturalist, upon whose evidence, but for his reputation as such, we would have bestowed very little notice, considering it, as we do, full of ignorance regarding the true nature both of the fish and the fishery.

Mr Little, being bred a stake-net fisher, and, in truth, the father of the stake-net system, the bias of his mind lay naturally that way; but it is deserving of remark, that when these engines were making their approaches to *his own* river, he opposed them most stoutly by every legal means in his power. He tells the Committee that if stake-nets are kept half a mile from the mouth of a river they will do its fishery no harm; supposing, of course, that when a shoal of salmon return from their migratory voyage and enter a frith, those which have the stake-net instinct in them steer for the stake-net banks, and the others for the rivers, so directly up the channel, that they diverge neither to the right nor to the left till within *half a mile* of the river mouth—when, tired of their monotonous course up the channel, or impelled by curiosity, they wander a little out of the channel, so that, if this last half-mile be kept free of machinery, it signifies not to the upper fisheries how full the rest of the estuary may be of it, there being no risk of the fish deviating from the channel till they come in view of port—that is of the river, the very part, we should think, where they would be most apt to keep the direct course; and therefore, says Mr Little, no stake-net should be allowed within that half mile. Nothing can be more conclusive than this reasoning, though it is somewhat at variance with the terror-argument of Dr Fleming, and with the *lousy* argument of the stake-net fishers, which would lead us to suppose that the salmon would then rush into the rivers at once.

Another witness examined in the Committee, a gentleman also of scientific pretensions, Mr John Steavenson, of Fortrose, tells us that salmon enter rivers just as the water happens to be to their TASTE. He says,—

"Salmon are extremely *nice*, and will only go into fresh water when it is *exactly* to their *taste*. For example, the Ness, Ewe, Shinn, and Thurso supply the earliest fish. The *reason is plain.*

These rivers are discharged from the largest lakes in Scotland, and consequently during the winter and early spring months send down water purified of all its *disagreeable* qualities, and in a state *liked* by the fish; while the late rivers, running from a mossy country, only *commence* to yield fish when the loch rivers above mentioned are beginning to *fail* (that is, when their water begins to become impure), indeed, when the *seasons* of some of them are terminated. In the Ness the season commences on the 10th of December legally, and the river immediately commences to give clean fish: they continue to increase in quantity till the first of March; they then decline gradually till the middle of May, and from that time till the end of July scarcely a salmon is taken in the river."

The water of this river must be shockingly impure during the summer months, when the water of other rivers is in its purest state. If Dr Fleming's plan of restricting the fishing season in all rivers to the summer months, that being the season when the engines of his friends fish best, were adopted, the river Ness would not add many salmon to the common supply. Mr Steavenson, however, as we said before, forgot to explain why, if the purity of the water is what induces salmon to enter the rivers at particular seasons, none enter them save *their own fish.*—Yet he tells us that the *seasons* of the early rivers are nearly over towards the month of March, which might show him that each river has its own season,—that is, that the fish of the different rivers are so constituted that they come to their respective rivers at their allotted time; the fish of some rivers beginning to come in November—while others do not come till March—and some not even till May. The salmon of the Shinn, which is one of the rivers to which he alludes, begin to come in November and December, through ice, and through miles of the very *impure* water of several other rivers, all collected in the common channel; yet they push their way through that impure water to their own river. It is not, as we have before remarked, after the salmon have reached the rivers, and have *tasted* the water, that the returning instinct commences its operation.—It must come into action long before then; or, to speak in the Quaker style, the spirit must move the fish of some rivers to quit their migratory abode in the ocean months before those of other rivers begin to take their departure. If this were not the case, the salmon of the late rivers would be all collected *en masse* at the mouths of their respective rivers, till the water became sufficiently pure, or to their *taste*, to induce them to enter. The fish of all the rivers come with regularity at their respective seasons, be the taste or quality of the water what they may,—all proceeding, like machines, obedient to their instincts: we observe the *facts*, and that is all we can know of the matter.

Mr Steavenson farther states—(we like to follow those scientific gentlemen, there being always something new and particularly edifying to be learnt from them)—

" I would wish to state, generally, that the fish taken in rivers are always of finer or inferior *quality* according to the state the river is in to *receive* them. When a river is in a state (that is, when the water is *exactly* to their *taste*) to induce fish, we get them of much finer quality than at a period when they do not enter so *readily*: they are apparently better *fed*—in better *health*, and in every respect superior fish."

This is a rare discovery. The feeding, and *health*, and quality, and appearance of the fish depend, not upon the parts they have come from, but upon the state of the water that is to *receive* them. *Cela est piquant!* It is no wonder if Mr Steavenson was a favourite witness of the Committee.

" The nearer (continues this poetical salmon-fisher) salmon are got to salt water, the finer is their quality; so much so, that any one versed in the state of salmon, would at once be able to pick out from five hundred head of fish those that had been more than two or three days in the river: indeed, I am not sure that I could not distinguish the fish which had been taken ONE MILE from the sea!"

Now, a salmon will run a mile in less than ten minutes or a quarter of an hour. What an admirable *coup d'œil* Mr Steavenson must have—*qu'il a le nez fin!* Baron Munchaussen himself could scarcely do more. Messrs Hogarth, Little, and Wilson—all great salmon-fishers—declare that it would be *impossible* to see any difference in a salmon that had been only a week in fresh water; but these men are mere drivellers compared with this salmon-fishing Mattadore, who can perceive the difference which running a mile in fresh water would make in the quality of the fish so clearly, that he could at once pick such a salmon out of 500 head, even though he had entered a water that was quite to his *taste*. We wonder how Mr Steavenson discovered *ce beau secret*. We suspect he must have found it from the old rascal of a seal who misled Mr Halliday—for the Highlanders believe that the fallen spirits have been sent into seals; and certainly it required something more than human—or, as our neighbours would say, *il fallait etre un peu plus que diable*—to have made the discovery ; which, *au reste*, was much of a piece with those of Messrs Johnstone and Co., relative to the movements of the fish *under water*, as stated in the Committee.

Mr Steavenson further remarks, that *there cannot be a doubt that salmon spawn in the sea.* Did the seal tell him this also? Perhaps, being a great sportsman, he has met with some wild ducks that build their nests in trees, while others make their nests on the ground, and has sagely concluded from thence that some salmon spawn in fresh waters, and others in the sea. We hope, however, that Mr George Hogarth, who has immortalised himself by rearing fry in a bottle, will convince him that he is mistaken ; for it were a pity that so great a naturalist, and so accomplished a salmon-fisher, should continue in error : but such is the lot of poor human nature ; the very greatest minds are sometimes mistaken.

The Committee, with their usual wisdom, further ask this witness,—

" Do you *consider* it to be the habit of salmon to seek the rivers during the summer months, or does any considerable proportion remain in the sea ?"

The proper answer to this question, we think, would be— that salmon seek the rivers during the summer months is proved by the *fact* that they are daily caught there by the river fishers ; whether any considerable portion, or what proportion, of them *remain* in the sea, it is impossible I can know. But Mr Steavenson replies,

"I am rather of opinion that the *greatest* proportion of them remain *constantly* in the sea."

"Do you mean that they remain in the sea *as matter of habit*—(O sage Committee!) or from any cause obstructing their progress to the river?"—"As matter of habit in *most* instances—(replies the equally sage witness)—but in some cases, because the river which they *happen* to visit is not in proper condition to receive them when they visit it. It is not *my* doctrine that each fish has its own river. If they meet with a river in a proper state to induce them to enter, the probability is that many of them will enter the river; but finding the water in a *disagreeable* state, they will either pass on the coast to another river, or they will leave the coast entirely, and remain at sea. It is within my knowledge that *very great quantities* have visited the mouths of many rivers I am acquainted with, and after having remained there for a *short* period of time—days in some instances, in others *weeks*, and I would almost venture to say *months*—they have left the mouth of that river, and gone to sea again, without having been seen ever more near it."

It is a pity the Committee did not put a few cross questions to Mr Steavenson regarding these *stationary* fish, which remained for *months* at the mouth of his river. They might, for example, have asked him—How do you know that these fish were *stationary*, and not passing fish proceeding to their own rivers, and replaced by others on the same course,—fresh salmon being then hourly coming on in constant succession, so as to render it impossible to distinguish the one from the other, in an element impervious to sight? If they were in the mouth of your river, why did you not run a net round them and catch them? If they were not near enough to do so, how could you *see* them under water? How could you know it was the *same* fish? It was not *possible* you could see them in deep water, or trace their motions; but, perhaps, you saw a fish leap occasionally out of the water: now salmon, in a frith or in the sea, never leap, except when proceeding on their course, and if you should see one leap out of the water to-day, and another to-morrow, having no mark upon them, how could you know it was the *same* fish, or that they were stationary, and not passing fish? Your whole tale relative to these stationary fish, which you could not possibly know to have been stationary or not, seems to us to rest on no evidence other than mere vague conjecture, unsupported by a single fact; for what fact could you bring forward to show what passes under water, or that it was the *same* fish, unless you had indeed some of Dr Fleming's balloons tied to them? and then you might no doubt trace their motions. Mr Steavenson, however, was not troubled with any questions of the kind, being a stanch stake-net fisher—whose evidence it would be by no means advisable to demolish.

In taking a view of the proceedings of the Committee, nothing strikes a man so much as the total absence, on the part of both the chairman and the witnesses, of all knowledge of the true nature, and instincts. and habits, and migratory movements, of the fish in question. The witnesses, indeed, could only answer such questions as were put to them; and they were in general so frivolous, and often so absurd, and even ludicrous, that it excites wonder how wise men and great legislators could put the like. We repeat, let the evidence of the stake-net fishers Johnstone and Halliday only be looked at: the complacency with which the same silly interrogatories are repeated every instant, to show off their system in the most captivating light, in order to impose upon the ignorant public; for what could be more ridiculous than to be constantly putting question upon question, which it was *impossible* any man could answer, relative to the motions of the fish in an element where no man, as we said before, could trace them for five seconds together,—and even about their *intentions!* Could anything be more farcical?

But while this was going on, the most important point of the whole, in so far as regards the public—viz. the obstruction and DANGER to navigation from the engines in question, was slurred over with very little notice. This point Mr Kennedy seems to have cautiously avoided, having put only a few questions on the subject to the stake-net fishers, whose answers, dictated by their own interest, he was sure of. One of the witnesses examined in the Committee had been prosecuted in a court of law for directing an engine of great extent, carried across an estuary (and which by overlapping another of almost equal extent, carried out from the opposite side, so that a boat in avoiding the one was thrown upon the other, thus rendering the navigation of the estuary so dangerous, that some of his people, who had been driven upon it in the night by the force of the tide, had nearly lost their lives), to be removed, without any application to legal authority, which in that country was so partial and corrupt, that any such application would have been useless, while the danger was immediate and pressing; yet Mr Kennedy, while he introduced the prosecution, with which (being a private matter) the public had no concern, in order to throw discredit upon the evidence of the witness as a river fisher and an enemy to stake-nets, which he himself so ardently patronised, never once put a single question to him for the purpose of *explaining* this danger—a circumstance deserving of particular remark; and when another witness, Mr Sheppard, stated that, in the bay of Cork, a boat's crew, consisting of eight men, had been DROWNED upon a similar engine, instead of farther examination into so material a point, the fact was *suppressed* in the proceedings, that it might not meet the public eye.

It has been maintained by the stake-net owners that those engines are useful to navigation. That they point out the banks to large vessels, may be true, though a single stake, or buoy, placed upon a bank, would serve the purpose equally well;* but no man will say that, if the coasts of the estuaries and the sea were barricaded with engines, of perhaps a mile in length, formed of strong stakes (and they must be necessarily of great strength, to support such a weight of heavy net, and to resist the action of the wind and tide), it would not prove both a serious and dangerous obstruction to the navigation of boats and small craft, by depriving them in stormy weather of the shelter of the land, and forcing them to go round them at the risk of being carried out to sea? Besides, at flood-tide these engines are nearly level with the surface of the water, and would not be observed by a strange boat till she came upon them, when she would be upset or swamped. Even Mr

* In 1816 the sloop Speedwell of Aberdeen, laden with timber, was driven upon a stake-net in the frith of Cromarty, and the stakes went through her bottom—which was the cause of considerable dispute between the owners and the underwriters.

Halliday admits in the Committee that, "*if the night is very dark you cannot see the nets.*" Accordingly, in a dark night the crew of the boat belonging to the witness we have mentioned, had, as we said, been lost upon one of these engines in the frith of Dornoch, clinging, after the boat was upset, to the stakes, till they were relieved. We wonder what the Lord Mayor of London would do if both sides of the Thames were covered with machinery of this description? He would no doubt order its immediate demolition; and are not the inhabitants in the remote parts of the kingdom entitled to the same protection? Perhaps not.

The only question seems to be, whether they may remove such dangerous nuisances *via facti*, or must involve themselves in endless litigation in the Courts of Law for that purpose. Mr Chitty, a celebrated English Counsel, as appears in the proceedings of the Committee, gave it as his opinion, that an obstruction of a much less formidable and dangerous description, which deterred the fish from ascending, might be legally removed by ANY person, as a public nuisance, without an application to a Court of Law; and Mr Saurin, late Attorney-General in Ireland, gave an opinion to the same effect regarding stake-nets, which was acted upon, and the engines demolished; but when the same thing, in one of the worst instances of the kind, was done in Scotland, the party was immediately attacked by all the satellites of the law, and fined, by a salmon-eating jury (who expected that, under the stake-net system, they would be saturated with salmon, and in whose eyes the LIVES of the people were of much less value than their own gastric functions), £100, with costs amounting to twice as much more—the honest and learned Judge never once telling them that an engine which was in itself *illegal* could not, upon the clearest principles of the law, be made the subject of a legal action; because, in Scotland, the clearest principles of the law are utterly disregarded when it is intended that an individual should be oppressed, a mere *pretext* being always sufficient.*

* Nay, let me tell you, professionally, that the legality of the mode of fishing practised by your friend Joshua is greatly doubted by our best lawyers; and if the stake-nets be actually an *unlawful* obstruction raised in the channel of the

Instead, however, of questioning the witness, as we have said, on the points relative to the danger to the lieges from the machinery in question, Mr Kennedy studiously avoided putting a single question to him on the subject, but brought forward the above action as a means of throwing discredit on his evidence, as a river fisher, and an opposer of his favourite system; and another witness, a man who knew no more of salmon-fishing than of naval tactics, and who was, besides, an inveterate enemy of the witness in question, was brought up 600 miles for the same purpose. This man, being asked,—" Did he consider stake-nets to be injurious to navigation?" answers, "No, quite the *reverse :*"—" Did he ever hear of a boat or other vessel being put to inconvenience or danger during their existence?" "Never in his life." "What was the breadth of the *channel* left unobstructed where the stake-net was demolished in the Dornoch frith?" "I should think FULL A MILE." Now the breadth, by measurement, was exactly fifty-two *yards*.

Such were the Committees under the unreformed *regime*. It is, however, to be hoped that, under the auspices of his present most excellent and patriotic Majesty, a different system will be adopted in all the departments of the State, and, above all, that the Augean stable, for it is truly such, of the Scotch law, will be cleansed and purified by the Commissioners appointed for that purpose.

_{estuary, an assembly who shall proceed, *via facti*, to pull down and destroy them, would NOT, in the eye of the law, be deemed guilty of a riot.—*Redgauntlet.*}

SECTION VIII.

CLOSE-TIME.

Let them alone: they be blind leaders of the blind. And if the blind lead the blind, both shall fall into the ditch.—ST MATTHEW.

THE present Act of Parliament relative to close-time, generally called Mr Home Drummond's Act, possesses *one* merit, namely, that of rendering the prosecution of poachers more simple and easy, which, in the present miserable state of chicanery and expense in the Scotch courts of law, is undoubtedly no small advantage; but this single merit is unfortunately accompanied by great destruction of private property, and by many absurdities most injurious to the fishery itself.

We shall not inquire what right Parliament has to interfere with the salmon-fishery any more than with any other species of *private* property. That the public has an interest in the fishery is granted: but has the public not an interest, and a much greater interest too, in corn? Why, then, does not Parliament lay down regulations for corn farmers? Why does it not enact that they must all, from Caithness to Cornwall—be the difference of soil and climate what it may—commence and end reaping their crops on the same day? That would be too ridiculous; every one would see at once the absurdity of it; yet this is the very thing that has been done relative to the salmon rivers, by placing the early rivers and the late rivers on the footing. The only difference between the cases is, that the one is less *palpable* than the other, because it is less understood and less visible to all; but, in point of fact, there is no difference whatever between them. If it be said that the individual interest of the corn farmer is a sufficient guarantee to the public, the same argument applies, with equal force, to the owner of a salmon river—that is, if his property were placed on the same basis of legal security with other property.

By this new act, the fishery begins on the 1st of February, and ends on the 14th September, in all the rivers in Scotland. We here trace the effects of the stake-net theory, by which no distinction is made between the early and late rivers, because, as stake-nets fish only during the summer months, the owners of these engines wished to bring the whole fishery as near their own fishing season as possible; and, accordingly, the candid Dr Fleming recommended that it should be carried on only from the 1st of May to the 1st of August. Neither this gentleman, nor the stake-net fishers, nor Messrs Drummond and Kennedy, seem to know that the winter months, as we said before, are as much *the regular fishing season* of the early rivers as the summer months are of the late rivers, and that the fish are then of by far the finest and richest quality; if Messrs Drummond and Kennedy do not know this, after all the fishing knowledge they acquired in the Committee, it is a great pity to see the whole salmon-fishery of Scotland at the mercy of such ignorance: if they do know it, how will they justify depriving the owners of the fishery and the public of so much valuable fish? For, by this Act, the owners of the early rivers, which the salmon enter clean from the sea during the winter, dare not touch them—dare not, in a country the "envy and admiration of all mankind," touch *their own* property, until it becomes useless—that is, until after the 1st of February, when the fish have lain so long in the fresh water as to have grown lean and discoloured, and *then*, our wise legislators tell them, they may kill them and send them to market. In the Tweed, and all the English and Irish rivers, this is not the case; for the new fish may be taken still in those rivers in their natural season, when they first make their appearance from the sea. The market is shut to Scotland alone, as if that degraded country were doomed by nature to be the victim of injustice, from her legislators as well as her courts of law; we say degraded, because we cannot conceive greater degradation of mind, than to submit, from *selfish* motives of prudence, to every injustice, without complaint, until apathy at length ends in a general *bouleversement*. Mr Kennedy attempted to extend the benefit of his act to Ireland, but the Irish members resisted it manfully. They could not, they said, accede to so much injustice—to such destruction of private property, without any advantage to the public ; so that the early rivers of that country escaped, while those of Scotland fell a sacrifice to the ignorance and pretension of the Scotch members, who, with a singular, but, we hope, not national, perversity, are always *forward* when nobody wants their services, and *backward* when the united voice of the country loudly calls upon them to stand forth in her cause ; and to whom acts of spoliation and injustice do not appear to have the same nauseous odour as to the more honourable minds of the Emerald Isle.

They know little of the nature of the salmon-fishery who do not understand that no injury *can* be inflicted upon a salmon river in which the public does not largely participate. If the owners of the rivers are prevented, by the interception of the fish by stake-nets, from improving them, fewer fish will be reared : if, by absurd and unjust acts, they are prevented from catching them in their proper season, the public are deprived of the finest part of the fish at a season when they are a luxury: in every view the interest of the owners of the rivers and of the public is inseparable. This great fishing truth, we repeat, is utterly undeniable. If the different constitutions of the rivers, as they were formed by Nature, be only attended to, it will be found that, under a proper system, as we before observed, a constant supply of fresh salmon might be obtained to the public throughout the whole year, instead of the three months recommended by Dr Fleming—one river ceasing to produce her fish just as another commences. In some early rivers, the new fish begin to come on early in November, in others in December, and in many in January and February. In those early rivers the fishery generally declines in April, when the fish of the late rivers begin to make their appearance, and in some of these they continue good till the middle or near the end of October—thus forming, from the admirable system of Nature, a succession of clean fish from one river or other during the whole year. Mr Sheppard states in the Committee, that the rivers Carragh, Lee, Bush, Newport, Bunderouse, and others, produce their new fish in November, December, and January, and decline towards April, giving few fish after that period; while the late rivers, such as the great Baillishannon River, the Earne, &c., do not begin to give fish till then; and Mr Little states that, in the Foyle, scarcely any are got till June; while, in the Shannon, the fishery, he says, is nearly *over* by the middle of May. In the Scotch rivers it is exactly the same. In the pamphlet published lately by Mr Fraser of Dochnalurg, to which we have already alluded, it is said that a greater weight of salmon used to be taken in the Ness *previous* to the 1st of February—that is, during the time none are at present permitted to be caught there—than during all the rest of the season. In the rivers Thurso, Shinn, and others, the salmon begin to enter in November, and the fishery almost ceases in April: in the Linshadder more salmon have, previous to the late Act, been caught in November, than during any other three months in the year; while, in an adjacent river, few make their appearance till May. In other rivers, such as the Spey, there are, as we formerly mentioned, both early and late fish, because some of their branches, or tributary streams, produce the one, and some the other, all of which go up the common channel. In the early rivers the fish accordingly go out of season, or become foul much sooner than in the late rivers. In many early rivers they are unfit to be taken after the end of July or the middle of August; while, in some late rivers they continue, as we said, good till after the middle of October. Mr Little states that the fish of the Dee are nearly a month earlier than those of the Nith, and are in bad condition nearly a month sooner; the close-time, therefore, says he, ought to be different in different rivers. Mr Buist states that the Tay fish fall greatly off in August, while those of the Esk continue good till the middle of October; and Mr Leach observes that, in the river Camel, the fish are in the best condition in October and November. All the most intelligent witnesses accordingly recommend a close-time suited to each river, which every man who studies Nature must agree ought to be the case. The Committee ask Mr Proudfoot, "Do you conceive that, in general, one law as to close-time would answer all rivers?"— "*I am far from that opinion.*" To the same question Mr Buist, the most intelligent of all the witnesses, replies, "Most certainly NOT;" and Mr Sheppard remarks, most justly, that it would be the destruction of the fishery, since the proper close-time for some rivers would comprehend nearly the whole fishing season of other rivers. But Messrs Drummond and Kennedy, steady to the stake-net principles, think that they can force the salmon of the early and of the late rivers to spawn at the same time; that what nature made different they can render uniform, and control Nature by an Act of Parliament!

And they accordingly fixed one general close-time for all the rivers in Scotland, from the 14th September till the 1st February. This we conceive to be the very essence of absurdity. Formerly the fishery ended in many of the Scotch rivers on the 26th of August, and even this was too late for the early rivers by at least a month; but, instead of fixing the close-time of those rivers on the 1st of August, the Act authorises the destruction of the fish—that is, of those which ought, unquestionably, to be left for breeders—to the 14th of September; and this addition of eighteen days to the period of destruction is called *lengthening* the close-time;—while, to make up for this, they add to close-time the winter months, when no fish go up the rivers to breed, for all the breeders of the season are then up, the clean, or new run, fish which come on at that time being all fish of the ensuing crop, which would not breed till the following autumn. The close-time is, therefore, thus *curtailed*, in fact, eighteen days, at the very period when a single day added to it would be of more importance than the whole winter months put together, without any benefit whatever to the fishery, except the saving of a few kelts, which might be otherwise sufficiently protected, and which can be no equivalent for the destruction of the fish, that ought to be reserved for breeders during these eighteen days, or the loss of the winter fish to the proprietors and the public.

To the owners of the fishery the injustice of the measure is too gross to require comment; and we do not think it likely that any great public measure which rests upon a basis of injustice can be ultimately successful. Injustice is always odious, whether it proceed from an individual, or from a body of individuals:* from a Scotch court of law, or from the British Parliament, or, in short, come from where it may. In the present instance, instead of benefiting the public or the fishery, it has a direct contrary effect, since it evidently injures both. We therefore trust that, under the existing enlightened administration, in whose minds we believe *honour*—that rarity in public men—prevails over the jobbing system by which the country, to the disgrace of the age, has been so long governed, and which has polluted all its institutions, particularly in Scotland, where public virtue seems to have been swept from the face of the country (if, indeed, it ever existed in it), some public-spirited individual in Parliament will move, at an early period, for the repeal of the present Act, and get another, founded in common sense, substituted in its room.

Why do our legislators suppose the Creator made early and late rivers? Was it that they should be put upon a *footing?* And does reptile man think he can alter the order established by Him? Every man of sense must see at once that the system of Nature ought to be followed? The only question is, *how* is this to be done? The grand evil in the salmon-fishery is the multiplicity of fishings, which begets so many contending interests, and makes each individual pursue a selfish system of destruction incompatible with the improvement, on a great scale, of the fishery. If anything could justify the violation of private rights for the benefit of the public, the owners of minor fishings should be made to sell their rights for a just equivalent, in order to concentrate the fishery as much as possible. If a whole river belonged to one individual, he might do with it as he liked. In such a river there should be no close-time. The owner of it would take care to keep it at all times full of breeding fish. He might make it like a game preserve, in which immense quantities would be

* We think to commit downright injustice is *ultra vires*, as the lawyers say, of any *human* tribunal.

reared. He would restrict the fishery entirely to a few stations near its mouth, and fish there constantly while clean fish appeared, supplying the public with new fish as they came on, even at the period the old fish were breeding in the upper parts of the river, without the smallest injury to the fishery; but a single upper heritor, were his fishery not worth £5 a-year, could put a stop to the whole plan. There are, accordingly, no rivers in the kingdom at present under so complete a system of improvement as those of the Duke of Sutherland in Sutherlandshire, under the able direction of Mr Loch, M.P. But this cannot happen in rivers which belong to different proprietors, and therefore a close-time seems absolutely necessary for such rivers—that is, such a close-time as a majority of the proprietors should consider best suited to each river; it being always understood, as we have already said, that the interest of the owners of the rivers and of the public is necessarily the same—viz. the production of as many fish as possible.

We believe that one of the reasons which influenced Mr Drummond in establishing a general close-time for all the rivers was, lest the salmon of one river might be smuggled to market as coming from another. But what did it signify, if the fish were *clean*, from what river they came? And foul fish never can be sent to market as clean fish, for their *appearance* would betray them at once. The deception would be seen at a glance;—as well might a man attempt to sell a black horse as being a grey one. In truth, no salesman would now venture to present foul fish at market: and if the fish are salted or kippered, we would defy any man to determine whether they were killed a week before or after close-time, or, indeed, to bring *legal* evidence to bear on the subject, since, as we said, salmon are as foul in some rivers in August as they are in other rivers in October. Besides, protection to one river can never be a good reason for injustice to the owners of another; and nothing can be more grossly unjust than to deprive the owners of the rivers Ness or Thurso of a great part of their properties, lest foul fish from the Tay or Tweed should be sent to market as coming from those rivers. If the Tay or Tweed are poached, let the proprietors be at the expense of a greater establishment of river-keepers, and not look to the annihilation of other properties to save their own purses. Here we have a striking example of Scotch principles of justice embodied into a British Act of Parliament at the instance of Scotch members :—Mr Home Drummond, as a check on the poachers in the Tay and Tweed, deprives the owners of the Thurso, Ness, and other early rivers, of half their properties, and the public of the finest fish.

In fact, very few foul fish have, at any period, been sent to market from the Scotch rivers, except from those parts of the Tay that are in the immediate neighbourhood of Perth. More, we believe, have been sent from the Tweed alone than from all the rivers in Scotland. It is in the remote parts of the rivers that the greatest number of foul fish are destroyed, and these parts are far from market. Nearly the whole is therefore salted and consumed in the families of the poachers. In the rivers which run through extensive mountainous tracts of sheep pasture, the shepherds are particularly destructive of the breeding fish. Lords of the wastes, they act as they please, for there is no eye to see them. The men who are employed by them in smearing their flocks are, accordingly, sent every night to kill the breeding fish, as food for themselves during the smearing operations, and many rivers are thus denuded of breeders. The proprietor of a river in the north sent some river-keepers among those worthies, but they could not procure a hut for shelter, and were obliged to return, the shepherds informing them, that their master had sent instructions, that if any of them should give a night's lodging to a river-keeper they would be discharged his service, which, on inquiry, was found to be true. Yet this master of shepherds is a magistrate ;—a distributor of *justice* and an encourager of *poaching*—no rare thing in a northern Scotch magistrate.

Many of the breeding streams belonging to the Scotch rivers run through lands which are not the property of the owners of the fishery, so that, unless the proprietors of the lands be forced to allow shelter-huts to be erected for the river-keepers, upon payment of a reasonable rent, it is evident that any enactments of the legislature for the preservation of the breeding fish will prove, in such rivers, entirely nugatory. A clause to that effect ought, therefore, to be introduced into any new act that may be passed on the subject; with power further to the owners of the fisheries to remove any falls or rocks which may obstruct the ascent of the fish. Such enactments would tend greatly to the increase of the salmon in all the rivers, and could do no injury whatever to the proprietors of the lands.

The fines in the present Act are greatly too low, and an absurd power of mitigating them is vested in the magistrates. In the ancient statutes, which contain many excellent regulations, none of the fines are under ten pounds, which was equal to as much sterling money of the present day. Scotch magistrates have often the weakness to prefer popularity to honour and duty. While the power of mitigating fines on illicit distillers was left in their hands, illicit distillation held steadily its course; but when that power, which of all men a Scotch magistrate is the last it should be intrusted to, was withdrawn, and the fines were raised to twenty pounds, an end was put at once to the evil.

We are no great admirers of the punishment of fines and imprisonment for all offences; a little variety would be better. To fine or imprison a poacher, is to visit the punishment on his *family* as well as on himself, which is not just. It would be better to make the carcase of the offender suffer for his fault. A good sound whipping on a market-day would, at the same time, be a salutary example to others. We recollect an instance of a prosecution of some poachers before two worthy magistrates—a worthy bailie, and a land-owner—when the fines imposed were so ludicrously trifling, that the poachers speared the fish again before they reached home. Had they been laid up a week with sore backs this would not have been the case.

We can, indeed, see no good reason why the stealing a salmon out of a river should not be declared *theft*, and punished as such, as well as the stealing of any other article. No man can deny a breeding fish, as we said before, to be infinitely a greater loss, both to the owners of the river and the public, than stealing a sheep off a common, or a pig out of its sty; yet the one is a capital offence, while the other is considered a mere trifle. It would be considered as a great hardship by farmers to be obliged to keep an expensive establishment of servants to prevent their corn from being stolen off their fields in the night; nor would trifling fines on the depredators prove any protection against such an evil. And it is the same with the owners of the rivers. These proprietors are unprotected, because the laws are inefficient, and the public participates largely in their loss.

There is one clause in those ancient statutes which directs that magistrates who fail in their duty should themselves be severely fined; and we believe that, during the time of one of the Jameses, a Lord of Session, whose decisions were reversed three times, was declared unfit for the office. The principle was founded in excellent sense. If judges judge often erroneously from incapacity, they are unfit for their office: if they do so from corruption of heart, or, what is nearly the same, from apathy or negligence, they are equally unfit. It is right that proper respect should be paid to the judgment-seat; but in Scotland this is carried a great deal too far. The judges are not the servants, but the LORDS, of the community, WHOSE WILL IS LAW, and who dispose of property, without a particle of responsibility. If Scotland had a manly, independent, and free press, the system could not have lasted so long; but no country on earth, as we said before, is less indebted to its press, and so it fares—for there is no other country more ridden and oppressed.

In Ireland, where the true nature of the salmon-fishery appears to be much better understood than by our Kennedys and our Drummonds, and where the salmon are consequently much more plentiful, the owners of rivers are not prevented from taking the new or clean fish when they come on from the sea, even during close-time, though the breeding fish are then protected in the upper parts of the rivers. This is as it should be, for the owners of the rivers have thus the full and natural use of their properties, which no legislature has a right to deprive them of,—all that is wanted from the legislature being mere *protection*. Thus Mr Sheppard states in the Committee,—

"The close-time is only applicable to persons *not* proprietors of the fishery.—The proprietors, by the existing Acts, are allowed the power of protecting the spawning salmon, and taking new fish when they offer."

"What then," the Committee ask, "is there to prevent a net catching fish in an improper state?"—"The *interest* of the proprietor."

"You say, you try for new fish in December?"—"Yes."

"And the fish are then coming up the river for spawning?"—"They are up the river a long way then, *i.e.* the spawning fish."

Here the Committee fell into the common mistake of confounding the fish of different seasons, for there are no fish coming up then to spawn,—the new fish which enter clean from the sea in the winter months, with small roes, being, as we said before, all fish of the *ensuing* crop or season, while those that are up the rivers belong to the last crop, or bygone season. The former would, of course, not spawn at the same time with the latter, which are then up the rivers spawning; but if not killed they would spawn during the ensuing autumn with the fish of the season to which they belong. Mr Little has fallen into the same error, when he considers these winter salmon as barren fish, not making the proper distinction between the fish of the two seasons, and confounding, as we have said, the fish of the incoming season with those of the past one.

Mr Sheppard farther states that—

"In the year 1774, a Bill was introduced into the Irish House of Commons, having for its object a *general* fence or close-time and weekly close-time, such as the two clauses now complained of, and the proprietors of the fisheries memorialised his Majesty on the subject, and he referred it to the Attorney and Solicitor General Thurlow and Wedderburn, who, after hearing evidence, *expunged* the clause, declaring that a general close-time was inapplicable, as a vast difference existed as to the periods of time at which new fish ascended the rivers—and that the clauses would be destructive of private property, and do no public good."

And it is this very obnoxious measure, condemned after hearing evidence, by such men as Lords Thurlow and Loughborough, which Messrs Drummond and Kennedy have, from a most erroneous notion of their own superior fishing knowledge, *forced* upon the owners of the Scotch salmon rivers; as

K

if the nature of the salmon in Scotland were different from that of those in Ireland. It ought to be always kept in view, that the regulation of close-time, and the suppression of poaching, are two quite different things. The close-time which existed previous to the present Act in Scotland has been observed these four hundred years, during the period the salmon-fishery was in its most flourishing state. The present proprietors made no application to Parliament to have it altered. The alteration has been made most unnecessarily by Messrs Drummond and Kennedy, and has been made greatly to the injury of the fishery, of its owners, and the public: all that was wanted by the proprietors being, as we have said, mere *protection* against poachers; and to this our legislators ought to have restricted themselves, if the legislative mania would have allowed them to do so, on points which they did not understand.

SECTION IX.

TROUTS—WITH REFERENCE TO THE SALMON-FISHERY.

> Des hommes sans loi, *et sans règle certaine*, faisant tout par leur volonté et par leur CAPRICE.　　　　　　　　　　　　　　　　　　　MONTESQUIEU.

THE trout is classed by Linnæus as a species of the genus *Salmo*: and as each salmon river has its own peculiar breed of salmon, so has each river, and stream, and lake, in which trouts are bred, its own variety of trout. If strangers to the salmon-fishery wonder that each salmon river should have a distinct variety of salmon, or each herring loch or bank, where herrings are bred, a distinct variety of the herring species, their wonder or scepticism must, we think, cease, when they find that even each trout stream, and river, and lake, not only in Great Britain, but, as Sir H. Davy remarks, in Europe, and, we doubt not, in the world, which are so infinitely greater in number than the salmon rivers, possesses a different breed of trout, varying from each other in size, shape, colour, quality, and flavour, and weighing, from the little trout in the streamlet to the great lake trout, as Sir H. Davy states, from less than half an ounce to sixty pounds—so boundless, as we before remarked, are the varieties in the works of Nature.

The quantities of trout produced in the Tweed, and in many of the Scotch rivers, particularly the Spey, are very great. In the river Ness many weigh from ten to fifteen pounds and trout have been caught in the river Shinn, in Sutherlandshire, which weighed thirty pounds. Some of these large trouts can only be distinguished from salmon by experienced fishermen. Formerly, when salmon were sold at a penny and three halfpence per pound, the trouts, in general, were considered of no great value, and in many rivers were given by the owners of the salmon-fishing as a perquisite to their fishermen, whose wages were less in consequence; but since salmon have been sent in ice to London, the trouts are packed in the boxes with them, and in many rivers form now a considerable item in the produce of the salmon-fishery.*

A question has lately arisen in the Court of Session relative to the *right* to these trouts in the salmon rivers, the proprietors of the adjacent lands claiming them as a *natural* pertinent of their lands; while the owners of the salmon-fisheries maintain, with somewhat more reason, that they are, on the contrary, a natural pertinent of the salmon-fishery, and have ever been possessed as such in all the salmon rivers in Scotland. The question, like every other relating to the salmon-fishery, is not without its importance to the public, as well as to the individuals concerned, from its tendency to add an additional obstruction to the improvement of the fishery, since, if it is difficult to prevent poaching even at present, when every person who is found prowling about a river is liable to a fine, by Mr Home Drummond's Act, how much more difficult would it be if a trout-rod were a sufficient passport to all poachers?

The destruction of young salmon by trout anglers is well described in the Committee.

Mr Little is asked—

"Do you consider that the destruction of salmon-fry by *anglers* is so great as to occasion any serious injury to the fishery?"—"I do think it is. There is an *immense* quantity taken out of the different rivers by anglers, in a state out of which they would be certain to grow to perfection. I have known even boys and children go and kill, in the course of an afternoon, twenty, thirty, and forty *dozen*. I have known one man kill thirty-five dozen in an afternoon; and if you take twenty or thirty in a day of those anglers, what an mmense number it comes to!"

Wilson—

"I have seen, from my own window, upwards of seventy or

---

* May 13, 1831, reached Billingsgate, from the river Spey, seventy boxes iced fish, whereof thirty were trout, the take of *three days*, which sold for *one hundred and forty pounds.*

eighty people angling *within the distance of half a mile* on the Tweed."

Proudfoot—

" There are a great many anglers who get liberty from gentlemen to go and fish—half-pay officers and others—who kill the salmon; but the greater number are of the lower orders. They say they have a right, by the law of Scotland, to kill *trouts*. I know some of those fellows who go about with rods in the daytime and observe where the fish lie, and come again in the night with nets and carry them away. This I know to be a *fact*."

The Committee ask Mr Little :—

" Do you know that poachers make angling a pretence for observing where the spawning fish are lying on the fords, in order to kill them during the night ?"—" I know that is frequently done. I have been told it by the people who practised it, and who afterwards engaged with us as keepers. We find that poachers make the best water-keepers. They tell me that it is the universal practice to go during the day and find where the fish are, and return during the night and kill them."

Before, then, a right which exposes the rivers to such *abuses*, and which must prove so detrimental to the salmon-fishery of the country, be established in law, it ought to rest on very CLEAR grounds indeed. When the amusement of angling is granted as a matter of courtesy—and it is seldom refused to respectable persons—it is not often abused; but if claimed as a right, there would be no check on its abuse, except by a constant recurrence to the courts of law, which, as law is at present administered in this country, is of itself an evil of no little magnitude. It is, therefore, a claim so destructive in its effects, that it ought to be resisted by the owners of the salmon-fishery to the uttermost. We may perhaps be told that the Scotch land-owners are too liberal-minded, too generous, too high-souled, to permit such abuses on their properties. No doubt they are so. They would give themselves a great deal of trouble, put themselves to a great deal of expense, prosecute even their *own* tenants, where they had no *interest* in the matter, or were on bad terms with the owner of the salmon-fishery, to preserve HIS property. They would never kill the salmon themselves by stealth even when heavy in spawn, for their amusement, or bribe the river-keepers to allow them and their friends to do so; and if a poacher sent them a present of stolen fish, they would not receive it; but these generous, high-souled, disinterested gentlemen, the very pinks of the Scotch magistracy, and of the Hidalgo race in the North, may be occasionally absent from the country, or too much engaged in their own affairs, to attend to the interest of others, and then the rivers would be left to their fate. The best protection of the fishery is to prevent the means of its abuse. Even the amusement of the land owners themselves would be promoted by it; for though a proprietor might be able to preserve his own side of a river, as all the pools are accessible from the opposite bank, he would not be a bit the better for it; whereas, under the general check of the owners of the salmon-fishery, none would be allowed to approach the river but persons of respectability.

It being, therefore, as we have said, a matter of considerable importance to the individual owners of the fishery, as well as to the salmon-fishery itself, as regards the public, all over Scotland, which depends so much on the protection of the rivers, to shut out as much as possible all *access* to poaching under a general system of trout-angling, we shall take a glance at the rights of parties as regards the *law* on the subject.

We have already remarked, that it is admitted by all lawyers that the first principle of the feudal law is, that the Sovereign is the original proprietor of all the lands and rivers in the kingdom, which, like any other proprietor to which the whole might belong, he might parcel out as he pleased. He might give a land estate to one man, the adjacent river to another, and the salmon-fishery of the river, if he chose, to a third, each having a right just to what he got, and no more. All this, we believe, no lawyer will dispute. It follows, then, that when a land estate has been granted, the grantee has a right to all that is within the bounds of the estate or grant, but nothing further: he can acquire no right beyond that, save by *prescription*. If the estate be bounded by a river, the water edge is necessarily the march. There the lands *end*, and with the lands his right.

To say that the lands on each side may claim half the river, as if they met in the middle of it, can rest on no principle, for the whole of the river continues the property of the Sovereign, or of the person to whom the Sovereign may have granted it; but if the rivers belonged to the lands, the Sovereign could not, in any instance, grant a river, for in NO instance could he have a river to grant; yet we know that in many instances the Sovereign *has* granted the rivers together with their salmon-fishery, distinct from the lands, with which, in law, they are considered to have no connection. The only right, then, of any kind, which the owner of the lands can claim in a river beyond the bounds of his grant, must be as a *servitude*, founded on prescription, as before remarked.

The right of the Sovereign to the trouts, as well as to the salmon, in those rivers, is beyond dispute; since, if all the lands and all the rivers originally belonged to him, all that was upon the lands and all that was in the rivers must have necessarily belonged to him also, according to the usual law of property. Lawyers no doubt tell us that salmon are *inter regalia*, and trouts not. They may just as well tell us that the whole kingdom is *inter regalia*, since all the lands and rivers of which it is composed are supposed to belong to the Crown, as well as the salmon. Why salmon should be specially considered *inter regalia* we leave to those to explain who can unravel legal inconsistency. We think it likely the salmon were looked upon in those days as SEA fishes, which only visited rivers occasionally, and that it was in that view they were considered, with the sturgeon and whale, to be *inter regalia*, without which they might be killed in the sea without a Crown grant; but this does not in the least affect the argument, or rather the principle, that, as owner of the rivers, the Crown had a right to the trouts in them, just as much as the owner of a land estate has a right to the nettles on the land as well as to the wheat, or to the shrubs as well as to the trees, that grow upon it. The right is founded upon a principle of property which is utterly unassailable.

The question then arises, To whom has the Crown given the right of these trouts? The owners of the land say, The trouts, not only in the streams *within* the bounds of our grants, but also in the rivers *beyond* the bounds of our grants, belong so naturally to the land, like the grass which grows upon it, that the one follows the other as a matter of course; besides, the Crown has granted to us the trouts in all adjacent rivers, let them belong to whom they may, by the words *piscationibus et pertinentibus* in our titles; and, moreover, trouts are *res nullius*, which belong to *nobody:* see upon what a firm and *consistent* footing our right stands! The owners of the salmon-fishery, on the other hand, say, The Crown has granted to us the trouts with the rivers, or as a part and pertinent of the salmon-fishery, of which they are undoubtedly a more NATURAL pertinent than of your *land;* and as we have *possessed* them, as such, for time immemorial, our right to them is indisputable. Such, we understand, are the arguments or grounds of right of both parties; but we must follow them more into detail.

First.—As to trouts being a *natural* pertinent of *land*, we think we need scarcely say much about the matter, since it speaks for itself. We may perhaps be next told, that partridges are a *natural* pertinent of water. "*Fishes* of any kind," says Stair, "cannot be considered as *annexis* or *connexis* of *land*, having so little connection with land." The right of a man to the trouts in the streams on his estate arises, not because fishes are a natural pertinent of lands, which is nonsense, in any way in which it is taken, but because they are *upon his property*. Besides, who else could claim them? Thus, a man has a right to the trouts in a pond—not because the trouts in the pond are pertinent of the adjacent *land*, but because the pond belongs to him; and, on the same principle, he has a right to the trouts in his streams.* The streams *belong* to him, and consequently the trouts in them. But this is very different from the trouts in rivers *beyond* the bounds of his lands or grant, though the Court of Session seem to have blended both together. Such rivers do

---

* Lawyers tell us that the game upon a man's estate does not belong to him, but that he may prevent others from committing a *trespass* upon his ground. Of what *use* is all this tortuosity! Would it not be more simple to say at once, the game belongs to the owner of the estate while it continues upon his property! His right to the trouts is stronger, because they do not leave the streams upon his estate.

not belong to him: they are separate property of the Crown or of the Crown's other grantees; and in no instance can the produce of one property, be it of what kind or description it may, be claimed as a *natural* pertinent of another property,— a rule which we hold to be without exception. There is not, in short, a single argument of common sense to support the absurd assertion that trouts are a *natural* pertinent of lands.

Next, with regard to the second point of the landowners, that not only the trouts in the streams *upon* their estates, but also in the salmon rivers adjacent to, though beyond the bounds of their estates or grants, have been conveyed to them by the Crown, in the words *piscationibus et pertinentibus* (which they conceive have a more imposing *sound* than the words "fishings" and pertinents), the first question that arises is, what is meant by this general expression of "fishings," which includes salmon and fish of every description, and which can, therefore, be only explained by the possession? The trout lawyers say it can mean only trouts, because salmon require a special grant. But if the word invariably means trouts, and trouts only, and was, as they say, intended to convey a special right to such, even without possession, was it not as easy to say trouts at once, instead of the general word "fishings?" Suppose the estate was situated on the sea-coast, where there are no trouts? Still, they tell us it means *trouts:* where there are none? Yes. And why not haddocks, which, if the Crown can, as they say, grant what is *res nullius*, may be meant as well as trouts? After all, the explanation of the word must depend, as we have said, on the *possession;* so that, *per se*, it can convey no right to any one kind of fish more than another, and to say that the word alone conveys the trouts *specially* in all the adjacent rivers, is an absurdity. The truth is, that the words *piscationibus et pertinentibus* are mere verbiage or words of style introduced into all titles, and which are of no earthly use, except as a title for prescription. This is so notoriously known that it is useless to deny it. But, granting that the expression really means trouts and nothing else, which no man could discover from the words themselves, still it can only mean the trouts in the streams and lakes *upon* the property, and nothing further. The titles, for exmaple, convey "the lands and estate of ———, with houses, biggings, muirs, mosses, woods, fishings, grazings, parts and pertinents," that is, the lands and estate, with the houses, muirs, mosses and woods *upon* the estate. The words are mere unnecessary tautology, which make a sort of parade in legal jargon, and convey nothing which a right to the estate would not itself carry. No man would be so absurd as to say that the "houses, muirs, and woods," mean woods, muirs, and houses upon *other* properties; and it would be just as absurd to maintain that any one word in the clause has a more extended meaning than the rest; or that while all the other words of the clause were confined *within* the bounds of the estate, such word ought to extend *beyond* the bounds of the estate, even if unsupported by any possession. If constructions were put on words contrary to common sense, there would be no end to the confusion in which rights would be involved. This construction of the word *piscationibus*, as meaning the fish in the streams that are within the bounds of the grant, is confirmed by the institutional writers on the Scotch law. Thus, according to

Stair—

"Cum aucupationibus, *piscationibus*, SIGNIFY privilege to kill fowls, *fishes*, and wild beasts ON THE FIAR'S OWN GROUND."

Bankton—

"The proprietor of the ground may no doubt fowl and fish THEREON."

Erskine—

"The right of hunting, *fishing*, and fowling WITHIN ONE'S OWN GROUND, naturally arises from one's right of PROPERTY therein."

Pertinents, again, are, in every instance, regulated by the *possession*. Indeed it would be an utter impossibility, in any case, to know what sort of a pertinent was meant under the general word pertinents, or to *discover* the undescribed pertinent, if any such there was, much more to establish a right to it, save by the possession. The word may, as we said, be used as a title for prescription, but in any other view it is absolutely useless. Accordingly, we believe there is not a single instance on record of a claim of pertinent being established save by the *possession*. It is a rule which admits of no exception.

Thirdly.—With regard to the assertion that trouts are *res nullius*, and trout-fishing consequently a common law right which all might exercise, it is evidently in direct contradiction to the other pleas of the landowners; for if trouts are *res nullius*, they could not be a natural pertinent of their *lands*, nor could the Crown have granted what did not belong to itself; but, as we said before, if the rivers belonged to the Crown, the trouts in the rivers must have belonged to the Crown also, and could not therefore be *res nullius*, for it would be contrary to all principle to say that the produce of any property can be *res nullius*, since, from the very nature of property, its produce must belong to its owner. We would like, too, to see the law which declares trouts to be *res nullius*. Where is it to be found? Let it be produced. Assertions are nothing. Any man may assert what he pleases to be law, but let the grounds for asserting it is law be shown. Let the precedent appear upon which it is founded. But the landowners, while they make this assertion to aid their claims, admit that the trouts belong originally to the Crown, for their principal argument is founded upon that principle, the *res nullius*, or common law right, being only brought in as an accessory thereto. Accordingly, they assure us that the right is a good *heritable* right as can be, flowing, as all heritable rights do, from the Crown, as a pertinent of the *land*, while the owner of this heritable right stands upon *terra firma;* but if he steps into a boat, this same heritable right immediately becomes a *personal* common law right, changing its character just as he changed his position: a sort of mongrel, demi-heritable, demi-personal, hermaphrodite right, of recent discovery among the *magi* of the Parliament House. Such are the *inconsequences* which too much ingenuity often leads to: it overdoes itself.

We have been trying to discover the grounds which gave rise to the vague notion which seems to be floating, like a dream, among the mists in the craniums of some lawyers, that trouts are *res nullius*, but could only trace it to a random expression of Stair, that "*white* fish, as cods, trouts, perch, &c.,

are common to mankind;" but Stair was in error, for trout and perch are not white fish, as cod, haddocks, &c. That sea fishes, which are produced in an element which belongs to none, should be considered as common to all, we can readily understand; but if the rivers were the property of the Crown, all they contained, as was said before, must also have belonged to the Crown. Perhaps Stair, not adverting to this principle, was somewhat at a loss how to dispose of the trouts, and accordingly, most un-Linnæus-like, threw them into the sea or white fish *res nullius* squad, which random act our lawyers of course consider as law, equal to an Act of Parliament. But an expression even of Stair cannot defeat a principle. Stair, however, made the *amende honorable* on the point in question, by admitting that a right to trouts might be acquired by prescription, which we scarcely think he would allow with regard to haddocks, or anything that was truly *res nullius;* but his random expression has afforded a *pretext*, which is quite enough to set all the mouths in the Parliament House a-barking. It is, at any rate, clear he did not consider trouts a natural pertinent of *lands*. Every one of the grounds, then, upon which the owners of lands rest their claim to trouts in salmon rivers adjacent to their estates, it thus appears, is untenable. They all, when investigated, slip from under their feet, without leaving as much as is worth the tail of a trout behind. Their claim has not, in fact, a foot to stand upon, except on the point of *prescription* alone, which they leave entirely out of their case.

It is amusing to follow the logical train of their arguments on the subject. For example—all the lands and rivers belong originally to the Crown, *ergo* the trouts in the rivers belong to the Crown also. But trouts are not, like salmon, *inter regalia; ergo* trouts do NOT belong to the Crown, But the Crown has granted a right to the trouts by the words *"piscationibus et pertinentibus;" ergo*, trouts DO belong to the Crown. But trouts are *res nullius; ergo*, trouts do NOT belong to the Crown. But trouts are only *res nullius* when fished for from a boat; *ergo*, when the fisher stands on land they are NOT *res nullius*, but a pertinent of land, or heritable property. But the same right cannot, in any circumstances, be *both* an heritable and personal right; *ergo*, the right is not a legal right, or a right acknowledged in law. But the right combines two rights which, separately, are legal rights; *ergo*, they are legal when joined, upon the principle that two blacks make a white, or two bad arguments one good one. But the trouts have been *possessed* by the salmon-fishers as a pertinent of the salmon-fishery, and as all pertinents are regulated by the possession, their right cannot be set aside until the law be altered. But a judge in Scotland can make new law, and he has ruled, that *fishes*, like trees, are so NATURAL a pertinent of *lands*, that no possession is at all necessary; *ergo*, the possession of the salmon-fishers goes for NOTHING, and you are a dunce. The logic is doubtless quite conclusive and unanswerable.

Let us now take a look at the other side of the question. Where a river itself has been granted by the Crown in property, together with the salmon-fishery, there can be no doubt of the grantee having a right to the whole fishes in the river, on the principle we have already stated, that a right to property carries a right to all that is contained in it, just as a grant of land carries a right to all that is upon it; nor is it more necessary to specify the trouts in the river than the trees or woods on the land. Where the Crown has granted, not the river itself, but the salmon-fishings of the river *with pertinents*, it may become a question between the grantee of the salmon-fishery and the Crown to which of them the trouts belong; but the matter is wholly *jus tertii* to the owner of the lands, who can show no right to interference in the matter. In this case, the owner of the salmon-fishery claims the trouts on two grounds; first, as being included in his *general* grant of salmon-fishing; and next, as having been always possessed as part and pertinent thereof. We shall make a few remarks on each of these grounds separately.

First.—A general grant of the salmon-fishings of a river must be held to include all the varieties of the *salmo* species in the river, and the trouts, some of which, particularly the bull trout, *Salmo eriox*, weigh more than 30 lb., are all classed by Linnæus, who is the best authority on the subject, as mere species of the *salmo* family. *Omne magus continet in se minus.* There is no restriction in the grant to the *Salmo salar*, or common salmon; on the contrary, the grant is as general as words can make it. If it were limited to the *Salmo salar*, it might be contended that the grilse was not included, for it has never yet been *legally* proved that the grilse is the young salmon, which Mr Little and other experienced fishers deny; while Sir H. Davy, who was a naturalist as well as an angler, maintains that the *trout* called the whiting, or finnock, is the young salmon. If, then, the general grant does not include all the species of the genus, and all the varieties of the species, which of them does it include? Does it include the grilse? or the finnock? If the finnock is, as Sir H. Davy states, the young *Salmo salar*, how can it be excluded? Or how be a pertinent of land? Or how could its destruction amid the other trouts be prevented, if the landowners were to get a right to the trouts? Besides, if, under the general terms of the grant, the whole species and varieties of the *salmo* family in the rivers have, as is the case, been *possessed* for time immemorial by the salmon-fishers, is not that sufficient in law to establish their right to them? We do not see how, after such possession, they can be deprived of them; nor, until it be clearly established, by proof, which of these fishes become the *Salmo salar* (if to the *Salmo salar* the grant shall be restricted), and which of them continue trouts (which it will be no easy matter to ascertain), do we see how any of them can be excluded from the general terms of the grant; nor what title the owners of the lands have to contest the point, it being a question entirely between the owners of the salmon-fishery and the Crown.

Secondly.—But, exclusive of the argument, that the general grant includes all the species and varieties of the *salmo*, the salmon-fishers claim the trouts as part and pertinent of the salmon-fishery, under the word *pertinents* in their grants; and if they have been possessed, as above stated, by them, for time immemorial, in all the salmon-fisheries in Scotland, both on the coasts and in the rivers, we do not see, we repeat, how such possession can be got over, since in all other cases of pertinent, prescription is *conclusive* on the subject. The whole case, therefore, on both sides, on this point, that is, as part or pertinent, depends upon the possession or prescription; but it is clear, that the same subject cannot be part and pertinent of *both* the lands and the salmon-fishings.

There has been only one case, we believe, tried on the subject, in the Court of Session, previous to the present time, namely, the case of Stirling *v.* Colquhoun, from the river Leven, about half a century ago; and it appears to have been so slightly and so imperfectly gone into, that it cannot be justly deemed a precedent, whereby all future cases should be regulated. If we look to the sentiments expressed by the judges, we find them all in contradiction with each other: no clear principle of law is laid down on the subject; and we search in vain for the *precise* ground upon which the decision was founded. The case was, however, a very plain and simple one. Sir James Colquhoun exhibited on his part a grant from the Crown of the salmon and *other fishes* in the river: his opponent produced no grant, but founded his claim upon the words "*piscationibus et pertinentibus*" in the titles of his lands, with immemorial possession. Sir James had, therefore, a clear right to the property of the trouts from the original general proprietor, subject to a *servitude* to his opponent, from prescription; yet the Court, while they acknowledged, in the fullest manner, the right of the Crown to the trouts, with inconceivable inconsistency, utterly disregarded the Crown's grant *aliorum piscium*, and bestowed the trouts upon his opponent as a pertinent of his lands,—but whether as a *natural* pertinent, or in consequence of the words *piscationibus et pertinentibus*, or from the admitted possession, does not appear. The Crown gave the trouts to Sir James, but the Court, superior to the Crown, gave them, in the face of the Crown's grant, to the other party. We shall cite the opinions of the Judges, and let the case speak for itself.

Henderland—

" THE CROWN HAS AN UNIVERSAL RIGHT IN LAND AND IN WATER, and in making grants it may reserve or convey the fishings. If Mr Stirling or his authors have *possessed* trouts, his right will be good."*

* This judge, it will be observed, places Mr Stirling's right upon the possession, or *prescription*. He does not once say, the trouts are a natural *pertinent of lands*,

Swinton—

"Fishing is *res nullius:* the right of fishing is properly by grant."*

Monboddo—

"I know nothing in this country which is *res nullius,* excepting the air," &c. †

Justice-Clerk—

"Salmon-fishings require grants; trout-fishings go with the lands as part and pertinent. It has been *said* that trouts are *res nullius.* In one sense they may be said *cedere occupante;* for, though I have a right to lands, it does *not* follow that I have a right to trouts swimming in the river, but I have a right to kill them. ‡ This right may be renounced, or it may be acquired by others. § The Crown

---

nor that they are *res nullius,* or a common law right, which does not require possession: on the contrary, he requires the possession, which is directly against the *res nullius* doctrine.

* This honest man calls the trouts, if by the general word "fishing" trouts are meant, *res nullius;* yet, with the same breath, adds, that the right to them is properly by grant, as if what was *res nullius,* as observed by Mr Erskine, could be the subject of a grant.

† This judge flatly denies that trouts are *res nullius;* in other words, that trout-fishing is a common law right, which every man may exercise, which is founded, and can only be founded on the *res nullius* principle; and it is not likely that if there was such law, this judge, and Lord Henderland, who admits the right of the Crown, could have been ignorant of it. The denial of Lord Monboddo, therefore, shows that it was NOT generally considered as the law.

‡ We have rare inconsistency here. His Lordship first says, that trouts are a *pertinent* of lands—and if they are a pertinent of lands, they are an heritable subject; yet in the same sentence he says, that the owner of lands has NO right to this *pertinent,* swimming in the water, but he may take and kill them, thus converting the pertinent into a *personal* right. If he meant merely that the owner of the land might kill the trouts, like others, he should not have called them a *pertinent* of the land, which shows great confusion of ideas. If, again, they are *cedere occupante,* and not *res nullius,* who is the ceding owner, unless it be the Crown? And if they are *cedere occupante,* how can they be a *pertinent* of the *lands?* Can anything be more ridiculous than all this?

§ If the trouts, as he said before, are a *pertinent* of the lands, and at the same time *cedere occupante,* not belonging to the owner of the *lands,* which is a contradiction in terms, who is it that might *renounce* this *cedere occupante* subject? Is it the owner of the lands, who, he says, has no right to them except as *cedere occupante?* He tells us the Crown has no right to them, and if they were *res nullius,* a right could not be "*acquired*" to them, any more than to cods or haddocks. To whom, then, do they belong? for he says, as already remarked, if I have a right to the lands, it does *not* follow that I have a right to the trouts (though a pertinent of the lands) swimming in the river? Do they then belong to nobody—this pertinent of *land?* but this would bring us back to

has no right to trout-fishing, any more than it has to fowling or hunting. The clause *aliorum piscium* is *unmeaning*. It could give no right which would not have attended properly although not expressed."

Monboddo—

"I cannot understand a grant *aliorum piscium* to mean *nothing*. In burns there may be a right to trouts as part and pertinent; not so in rivers; there must be a grant." *

Braxfield—

"Fishings may be separated from lands, then the Crown will have a right to all fishings; † but if the Crown feus out *cum piscationibus*, and with parts and pertinents, this will carry inferior fishings."‡ A grant *aliorum piscium* may be effectual by prescription.§ Sir James

the *res nullius*, and to the question, who is it that is to *"renounce"* this *res nullius?* or how acquire a right to it? It seems to us all a tissue of absurdity. A pretty precedent, truly, for regulating all future cases on the subject. He considers the clause *aliorum piscium* unmeaning, as it could give nothing to the lands but what they already possessed—that is, as *pertinent*, which was " *cedere occupante*," and to which the owner of the land had " NO right, when swimming in the water ! ! ! "

* In other words, that the trouts in the burns or streams *upon* a property belong to the owner of the property; but that in rivers adjacent to the property he must have a grant—consequently they are not a natural pertinent of the lands, any more than they are *res nullius* or *cedere occupante*. This judge and Lord Henderland appear to be the only consistent men, as we noticed before, among them. They admit directly the right of the Crown, which the Justice-Clerk, as we have just seen, as directly denies. Which of their opinions are we to consider LAW?

† Has the Crown a right to fishings before they are separated from lands? We thought *both* the one and the other belonged originally to the Crown, and that it could convey them together or separately: it is not easy to understand what his Lordship means, or to make sense of his speech.

‡ If, as he says, the Crown has not a right to fishings till *after* they are separated from lands (from which they are separated by nature), how could the Crown grant a right to them *with* the lands by the words *piscationibus* and parts and pertinents? He, however, admits the right of the Crown, which the Justice-Clerk denied, and thus virtually rejects the *res nullius* and *cedere occupante* doctrine.

§ Why should not a grant from the Crown *aliorum piscium* be as effectual, without prescription, as a grant *cum piscationibus*, the one being an *express* grant, the other, as we have said, mere words of style? Stair, and the other writers on the law, as before noticed, say that *piscationibus* can only give a man a right to fish in the streams on his *own* ground, but this judge makes no distinction, whether he meant any or not.

Colquhoun might have acquired a right to trout-fishing by prescription, but he has not; he has been wont to *catch* trouts, but not to exercise a trout-fishing.* He is not entitled to catch trouts with a net appropriated to that purpose."†

Eskgrove—

"Lands and fishings are understood to be the right of the Crown originally. Grants from the Crown *cum piscationibus* carry NOTHING, unless explained by POSSESSION. Such a grant might imply that the Crown was not to resume it. Heritors may fish trouts *ex adverso* of their lands; but I doubt whether they can interrupt those who may choose to fish from a boat."‡

Such, then, is the only precedent on the subject. Each learned judge not only contradicts most learnedly his neighbour, but contradicts himself. All seem as if playing a game at cross purposes, more like a parcel of schoolboys than a set of grave judges uttering the dictates of wisdom, and founding their judgment upon a clear principle of law. Only one of

---

* Sir James acquired his right by his grant from the Crown. The distinction between *catching* trout, and exercising a trout-fishing, is nothing but quibbling. Did Mr Stirling do more than *catch* them? If it is meant that Sir James did not keep a regular trout-fishing establishment, it is what has never been kept anywhere, even yet, and certainly was not by Sir James's opponents. The trouts in those days would not pay a tenth part of the expense of such. They have been always, and are still, killed by the *salmon*-fishers. This judge appears to have looked upon Sir James's side of the question with a very jaundiced eye. The whole of his remarks show it.

† Here was another gross instance of partiality, for this was allowed by the Court to the other parties—to persons who, in fact, had no right, and denied to the Crown's grantee!

‡ He admits that the words *cum piscationibus* carry nothing without *prescription*, and imply only that the Crown was not to *resume* it. Where did he ever hear of the Crown *resuming* a grant once made? When he says an heritor may fish *ex adverso* of his lands, we presume he means after he has acquired a right by *prescription*, as he before remarked. He does not say that the man who fishes *ex adverso* of the boat, requires prescription, like the man with *piscationibus* in his titles on land, nor that he needed a right from the Crown, though he admits the Crown to be the original *proprietor* of the fishings. The right is an heritable one to the man on land, derived from the word *piscationibus* and his possession; but to the man in the boat it is quite a different thing—or what our trout lawyers call a common-law right, a mixture of *res nullius* and *cedere occupante* flowing from the Crown to the one, and from the unknown ceding owner, supposed also to be the Crown *incognito*, to the other. All this exposition of the law is altogether amusing.

them, Swinton, calls trouts *res nullius*, which Lord Monboddo, who, notwithstanding his notions about tails, seems to have been the best judge among them, flatly contradicts. Another, the Lord Justice-Clerk, considers them *cedere occupante*, but he stands alone in his opinion; and a third, Eskgrove, *doubts* whether a man could be prevented from killing them in a boat. It is quite clear, from the confusion of their ideas, in which the most opposite doctrines are jumbled together, that they could find no particular law which bore on the subject, or which rendered a right to trouts different from any other question of an heritable nature that might come before them, and they ought, therefore, to have put it on the same footing, and judged it by the same rules, as any other heritable right. The whole case was clearly a simple question of servitude or *prescription*. We do not think that Sir James Colquhoun got anything like fair play on the occasion, with his grant from the Crown *aliorum piscium* in his hand; for while his opponent, with, we may say, no grant at all, was allowed to kill trouts with nets, Lord Braxfield expressly declared that Sir James, the Crown's grantee—the legal owner, in fact, of the subject—should *not* be allowed to take them with a net appropriated to the purpose.

This right of trout-angling is evidently a right which CANNOT be exercised, which cannot even exist without injury to the salmon-fishery; and it requires a greater strength of reason than we are possessed of, to conceive the LEGALITY of a right *which cannot be exercised without injury to superior rights*. It appears to us in the shape of a *legal* right, as an anomaly, which we can no more understand, than we can understand how a right can be *both* an heritable and a personal right at the same time. It is a right, *per se*, of which there is not an example in the whole catalogue of our rights—a right *sui generis*, a nondescript, which has its fellow only in the bond of honest Shylock, who might take his pound of flesh, if he *could*, without a drop of blood—a right legally to do what one *cannot* do legally; a right, in short, founded in no KNOWN law, and contrary to all justice. Such is the mongrel, demi-heritable, demi-personal right granted as a NATURAL pertinent of *land*, without either title or possession, or a particle of legal ground on which it can rest, save the *sic volo* principle of the Court, opposed to the IMMEMORIAL POSSESSION of the owners of the salmon-fishery.

Such is the present state of the Scotch salmon-fishery. It is as clear as that two and two make four, that the fishery can only be improved in two ways: first, by rearing as many fish as possible, which can only be done by incessant attention on the part of the owners of the rivers and next, by preventing the fish from being killed in such quantities, before they reach their proper growth, by over-fishing; and in both particulars the Court of Session seems to be doing all in their power to depress the fishery, by cutting up the rights of the river heritors, by whom alone it can be improved, and by extending the over-fishing system on the coasts. It seems to be running a race against the fishery, as if for the express purpose of preventing its improvement, and so has fared with it; for in the very first article of the Report of the Committee of the House of Commons, it is stated that the fishery has for many years been decreasing, and is still decreasing so rapidly, that unless means be adopted to prevent its further decrease, the loss to the public must be very great. In the Provincial or Sheriff Courts, the same system seems to be followed. In a recent case, the tacksman of a river was foiled in his attempt to prosecute a poacher, who had been fishing in the night with a fixed or hang net, declared *illegal* by repeated decisions of the Court of Session,* on the ground that the matter was *jus tertii* to him, according to the doctrine recently promulgated, and he had *eighteen* pounds of expenses to pay for making the attempt; † and on another occasion, a reservoir, which the tacksman had made for keeping the fish alive, in order that they might be sent to market in ice, instead of being pickled, was, after having been peaceably possessed during *eight* years,

---

* Duke of Queensbery v. Marquess of Annandale, 19th November 1771. Dirom v. Little, 25th February 1797.

† Qu. Who has the right to bring offenders against the law to justice ?

most wantonly ordered to be demolished by the Under-Sheriff, whose jurisdiction only extended to *seven* years, though its legality was neither struck at by the statutes, nor by any decision of the Court ; yet these instances of judicial oppression were quietly submitted to, as a less evil than entering into that gulf of litigation, the Court of Session, in quest of redress ever uncertain, and always accompanied by the most ruinous expense. In short, it seems to be the fate of the salmon-fishery to have obstructions thrown in the way of its improvement in every quarter; and this is likely to continue to be the case until the true nature of the fishery be better understood, when it is possible that the interest of the *public*, if not justice to individuals, may force the Courts of Law to adopt a different system or mode of procedure.

In the mean time, we would strongly recommend to the owners of the rivers to join, and try another SEA stake-net case, say from Montrose, and another *jus tertii* case from somewhere else, for the purpose of having the law on these important points fully settled upon proper principles, and set finally at rest.

P.S.—It was forgotten to be stated in the proper place, that if we appeal to NATURE for the termination of the sea or of a river, we may find it. The attraction of the moon *raises* the sea above its *natural level*, and produces the tidal wave. Now it appears to us that the line of coast, the margin of the sea, should be that which the sea exhibits when there is *no external cause* operating upon it. Were the attraction of the heavenly bodies removed, the margin of the sea would be the line shown at what we call low water, which is in reality its *natural* margin. This doctrine, if it have not the ingenuity of those of Messrs Jardine and Steavenson, has at least truth and simplicity and nature on its side ; and we venture to state that, when our forefathers made the cruelly misinterpreted laws relative to the salmon-fishery, they had the very same view of the matter. For, as before noticed, they knew that cruives *could not* be set in the sea, nor yairs in rivers; and hence they regulated cruives in fresh water, and prohibited yairs where the tide ebbs and flows, because it is the ebbing and flowing of the tide, *and nothing else*, that enables yairs to catch fish, and destroy the fry of *all* fishes which are not found in rivers. If it be desired to preserve the fishery, all estuaries should be declared rivers to a certain distance from the rivers which flow into them.

APPENDIX.

DO GRILSE GROW TO BE SALMON.

M. I have frequently heard you remark that a grilse is a distinct fish from a salmon, though of the same family.

H. Yes ; its instincts in some respects are different, though its habits are precisely the same ; and this is the reason why superficial observers have considered them one and the same fish.

M. Explain to me how you have arrived at that conclusion, so opposed to the theory generally received ?

H. The answer to your question can only be developed by degrees, as we proceed with the examination of the subject.

M. Before proceeding further, I should like to hear your definition of instinct, a word frequently used in connection with animals, but which seems to me to be but little understood ?

H. Instinct is a law of nature which influences animals with systematic regularity, and without the aid of any reasoning faculty in themselves, to the exercise of those functions bestowed upon them by Providence, in the same mysterious manner as the needle of the mariner's compass is influenced by an invisible attraction, always pointing to the north whichever way the compass is placed ; and it would be just as impossible for a salmon to alter its physical shape at will and become a shark, or any other animal, as to deviate from its instinct, as the

Almighty Power that created the animal exercised an equal amount of omniscient knowledge in devising an instinct for its guidance and functions. Instinct is, therefore, unerring, or the word should be expunged from our dictionaries.

M. I am perfectly satisfied with your definition of instinct; tell me now how it influences salmon differently from grilse?

H. As the human eye cannot follow the motions of fish while in the sea, their habits can only be ascertained by watching them during their annual migrations to the rivers, where they are completely within the reach of our observation. Experience then shows us that salmon, impelled by their instinct, leave the sea for their home or rivers in winter and spring; whereas the grilses do not leave the sea for the rivers until summer, clearly showing that the one is a spring, and the other a summer fish. Another difference, which I shall explain more fully hereafter, is, that although I have a hundred times made inquiry on the subject, I have never yet heard any old Highland poacher assert that he had seen salmon and grilse spawn promiscuously; but, on the contrary, that he invariably found either two grilse or two salmon performing that operation. My own experience as a fisherman for thirty years goes to corroborate the same fact.

M. If instinct is unerring, how do you account for some rivers producing salmon earlier than others?

H. Instinct has nothing to do with the nature or the circumstances connected with early or late rivers; but in the seasons of their migrations, instinct directs the fish of each river to itself; and were all the fish in the sea suddenly to become blind, every fish would proceed directly to its own natal river, passing all others, regardless of their taste or temperature, still impelled onwards by its instinct, which does not cease operating from the time the fish left the ocean until it had reached its destination; the only inconvenience it would experience from blindness being, that it could not escape from its enemies, or procure its food.

M. If, then, the instinct in salmon leads them to return to their natal river, passing all others, how do you account for the fact of fish, recognised as belonging to a certain river, being caught at or near the mouth of another river at some distance from its own ?

H. It is admitted by all parties that salmon, when leaving their rivers, migrate to the north. It is therefore not surprising to find salmon intercepted in the innumerable traps laid for them when they return on their way south. For instance, the Tweed bull-trout, commonly known as the "black tail," a very conspicuous fish, may be intercepted on its way from the north, but it has never yet been seen to the *south* of the Tweed ; and if its instinct was not perfect, the Dee, Don, and other rivers, by this time of day, would abound with it, as the Tweed does. I may here hint my belief, that it will prove impossible ever to succeed in propagating salmon in the Australian rivers; and this in consequence of the inflexible instinct always drawing them in their migrations towards the north pole. Were this not the case, all the rivers in South America, Africa, and India, would have salmon in them, making an annual migration to the *south* pole. Thus, had nature so decreed it, there would have been salmon in the southern as well as in the northern hemisphere.

M. Now that you have brought salmon back to the rivers, what is their condition and general appearance ?

H. They have a beautiful silvery appearance, and are in high condition. Before ice was made a substitute for boiling and kitting salmon, it was proved by the quantity of oil—a perquisite of the salmon-boiler—skimmed off the boiling kettles, that spring fish invariably produced more oil than summer fish ; thus showing that early fish are superior as food to late fish. It was also proved by those boilers, that they generally had little or no food in their stomachs ; that every salmon contained either roe or milt, and that the quality of the fish decreased in an inverse ratio to the growth of the roe, and as the spawning season approached. A curious fact, relative to the roe in grilse and salmon, and proving in a great measure my assertion that they are distinct fish, is, that when the grilse appear in May and June, their roe is in precisely the same stage of growth as it was in the salmon when they made their appearance in the rivers in January, from which time their roe has been gradually progressing in size; so that in May it may be called half-grown, at the same time that the roe of the grilse is so small as to be scarcely perceptible. As, however, the two fish spawn at the same time, it follows, as a natural conclusion, that the roe in the grilse requires only half the time which that of the salmon requires to bring it to maturity; which shows a decided dissimilarity in their organisation.

M. We have not yet said a word about grilse; where are they all this time?

H. The instinct of the grilse leads them, in May, to perform their annual migrations on their way to the rivers, as at this time of the year the salmon-fishing in all quarters is virtually at an end,—their season having gone by, and grilse taken their place,—though they are not seen in large numbers until June and July, with but comparatively few salmon intermixed with them. Hence it is a common remark amongst fishermen, that though the salmon-fishery may be bad, still the grilse-fishery may be productive, each fishery varying in quantity to correspond with the favourable or unfavourable season in which they were spawned,—clearly showing two distinct fisheries and nature of fish.

M. Is that your only reason for supposing that grilse do not grow to be salmon?

H. No. Some people suppose that the smolts of a few inches in length, that go down to the sea in March, return again to the rivers in May, after an absence of only two months, as grilse of an ordinary size, from four to seven pounds' weight. But my belief is, that when the smolts that required twelve months to arrive at the size of from four to five inches in length, and apparently in good condition, as their appearance is round and plump, will necessarily require a longer time than two months to arrive at the size of from four to seven pounds' weight, notwithstanding the virtue in salt water. But the absurdity of the theory consists in the assertion that the *smolts of salmon*, going down to the sea in company with the smolts of grilse, also return from the sea under the denomination of grilse,—thus dispossessing the sea entirely of a crop of salmon for next year's supply; as it necessarily follows that, if instinct operates on an individual salmon or grilse in bringing it back to the rivers in summer, it must operate on the entire body collectively. So that the illogical and vulgar theory of leaving to the option of some of the fry to return to the rivers, while their companions remain in the sea, and apparently with no object in view beyond the very considerate one of benefiting the spring fishermen, must be dismissed by the naturalist as being in direct contradiction to the laws of nature and the grand migratory system.

M. Under that impression, you maintain that salmon and grilse remain in the sea a longer time than is generally supposed?

H. Yes. The fry of salmon, as well as that of grilse, are a year old before they quit the rivers. I believe they remain another year in the sea—perhaps longer—when the instinct of salmon moves them to quit the sea in spring, and some in the latter months of winter, on their way to the rivers. The instinct of grilse does not operate till the beginning of summer, when they commence their journey also to the rivers—all for the purpose of propagating their kind, precisely in the same way as do the swallows, lapwings, teal-ducks, and all gregarious creatures, whether birds or fishes.

M. Have you any other proof in support of your theory?

H. One simple and palpable fact, which any ordinary observer might have remarked is, that grilse in May weigh from three to five pounds; in July, they are met with as large as from ten to twelve pounds; and instead of finding them, in August and September, grown to the size of sixteen or twenty pounds, which would be but natural if they continued to grow to become salmon, they apparently begin to grow backwards; as in October we have them as small as we had them in May, not growing one inch larger from that time till they return to the sea in March and April as kelts. Before quitting this subject, I may as well mention another fact, which of itself seems to me conclusive; and that is—that there are some rivers in Scotland which produce salmon with but very few grilse. Such is the Shinn, in Sutherlandshire, whose fishing season is considered virtually finished before the time when grilse make their appearance; and so few of these frequent that river that they are not calculated upon as part of its commercial produce. Other rivers, such as the Oykell, produce very few salmon, and these of indifferent quality, but depends almost entirely upon its grilses, which it produces in shoals. This is also the case in a very marked degree in the rivers in Ireland.

M. Have you at any time marked grilse with wire or otherwise for the purpose of ascertaining whether they grow to be salmon?

H. Upwards of thirty years ago I marked a number of grilse by tying a wire round their tails. Three years afterwards some of them were caught with the wire round the tail, and grilse still. I have read of grilse being marked by other people, and some of those grilse afterwards caught weighing fourteen pounds, and called salmon. Until, however, grilse are found to have grown to be salmon beyond that weight, I must still continue to believe them to be grilse, though mistaken for salmon, as fish *allowed* to be grilse, weighing fourteen pounds, are said to be caught in the month of July; particularly as my present object is to enunciate principles, and not to controvert the results of ill-devised experiments, such as the Stormontfield ponds, or markings at any other places or rivers, of salmon or smolts. Similar markings have been practised, to my knowledge, for upwards of thirty years, without arriving at any very practical conclusion.

M. How then do fishermen distinguish salmon from grilse, if they have no distinctive peculiarities, and are not always regulated by weight?

H. They affirm that a grilse has a younger appearance than a salmon; but without any external guiding index there can be no certainty in determining a point where one man's opinion is as good as another's. The only distinction I could ever ascertain is, that the tail-fin of a grilse tapers off to a finer edge than in the salmon: this distinction is observable in the smolts also.

M. How do you account for the variety in size of grilse, some being so much larger than others?

H. You might as well ask me to explain the difference of size in salmon, which varies from six pounds to fifty pounds, and sometimes sixty pounds. The only way it can be accounted for is, that the large salmon are the produce of rivers or their tributaries so formed by nature as to produce a large-sized fish, other rivers producing a salmon of a small size. The same law holds good in rivers producing grilse; and although there are occasionally very large grilse met with, the aggregate size of one year does not vary much with that of another throughout the season. Hence it is that we have the average of six pounds' weight in May, and a similar size in October; but if grilse grew to be salmon, and as rapidly as is generally supposed, we should have no grilse in October, but all salmon.

M. Suppose now that such of the grilse and salmon as have escaped the various snares, which the ingenuity of man and the watchfulness of the fishers have placed in their way, have arrived in the rivers for the purpose of spawning, when do you think that operation takes place?

H. From experience and induction, I believe that the process of spawning takes place chiefly in the month of November. From experience, because year after year I have seen them crowding the fords, spawning in that month; which feature is particularly observable in the tributary streams falling into a loch, wherein they are not seen throughout the year, except in the month of November, for the purpose of spawning, and then they are to be seen in multitudes. This is the case in a remarkable degree in Loch-na-Shalag and Loch Maree, on the west coast of Ross-shire. The same instinct is very conspicuously exemplified in the char, a beautiful and highly-flavoured fish, found in many Highland lochs, and particularly numerous in the above-mentioned Loch-na-Shalag, but which, from its habit of remaining in the deepest parts of the loch, can be but seldom caught by the fisherman. It is a well-known peculiarity in these fish, that at an appointed time, in October, they quit the lochs, keeping clear of intermixing with the innumerable families of trout, and betake themselves in shoals and nations, with stereotyped regularity, to the tributary streams, for the purpose of spawning. As soon as this is accomplished they fall back again to the loch, not leaving it until that time next year, when instinct again comes into action, compelling them to go through the same process. By induction, because the month of November, by the laws of nature, is decidedly the month peculiarly fitted for that operation to suit the instincts and habits of the fish, as well as to guard against the severity of December frosts; as when the fords are bound up with ice in winter, the progress of spawning would be utterly put a stop to. In early rivers the salmon come to them early in the season, and will, as a natural consequence, commence probably to spawn a fortnight earlier, and in late rivers a fortnight later; but in no river will the spawning operation proceed when the river is covered with ice; and Nature foresaw this contingency when it appointed the month of November. Besides, the uniform progressive growth of the roe towards maturity, gradually increasing from January in the salmon, and May in the grilse, shows that of necessity it must be deposited in November as ova in the fords, for if it be delayed long beyond that time it will become unproductive.

M. Are there any peculiarities connected with the process of spawning?

H. The same instinct prompts fish to prepare a place in the gravel to deposit their ova that bestirs a bird to prepare a nest for its eggs; the only difference being that, living in opposite elements, their mode of action must be different, inasmuch as the bird builds its nest with its beak in carrying the materials, and the action of the body to fashion its shape; whereas the salmon chiefly depends on the action of the water in assisting the progress of its operation.

M. That is the reason, I suppose, why salmon select fords or the running stream, instead of still water, as most suitable for their purpose?

H. Precisely so: two salmon, a milter and a spawner, instinctively select a suitable situation in a ford, and by a mutual impulse commence to agitate the sand by a vibratory action of their fins, tails, and bodies, thereby stirring up the gravel, and almost simultaneously throwing themselves by a muscular exertion of their tails upon their sides, and by gentle contact emit their ova, which is carried off by the action of the water, and gradually subsides immediately behind them, mixed up with the gravel. This operation is carried on for a fortnight by each pair of fish, if they are not disturbed, when the process is completed. The general opinion is, that first the fish dig a hole, and deposit their spawn therein. If those people were only to give the subject a moment's serious reflection, they would at once find that such a supposition could not in point of fact ever be realised; as, with every additional agitation of the gravel in the bottom of the hole, the roe would be thrown out of it along with the gravel. By the time the spawning operation is ended, a hill or molecule of considerable size has gradually accumulated immediately behind the hole or bed excavated by the fish, and any person taking the trouble of examining that mound will find the ova mixed up in it; and were we as conversant with the laws of hydraulics as Nature is, I have no doubt we should find the ova more secure in mounds immediately below the excavation, than if deposited in that excavation. Salmon do not spawn in pools, because, without the action of running water, they could not cover in their ova,—without which precaution it would be left exposed to be dispersed by floods, or swallowed up by other fishes. Running water is not, however, essential to the vivification of the young fish, for we find that the ova of carp, breams, barbel, and trout that inhabit ponds, come to perfection in still water.

M. I have read in a pamphlet that the salmon dig the spawning hole or bed with their "*snouts.*"

H. By its physical conformation a naturalist would at once pronounce that it is an impossibility for that fish to apply its snout to a digging purpose. In the first place, the creature has no neck, and consequently has not the power of moving its head up or down without a corresponding movement of its entire body; and, even if the fish retreated a few yards, *reculer pour mieux sauter*, to give it an impulse, it would still be necessary for it to raise its tail out of the water at an angle of 45°, to enable it, like a pick-axe, to knock its snout against the gravel, or, for anything the poor creature knew, against a stone. Had a salmon a snout like a pig, with joints in its neck, we might then come to the conclusion that those necessaries were provided by Nature for the purpose of digging. In the second place, the cartilage of the nose is so tender that it could not, with any degree of comfort to the possessor, be applied to such violent shocks without disturbing its equanimity, and disgusting it with its work, however amusing it might be to lookers-on from the bank of the river. Besides, the gravel disturbed by the snout would enter the fish's mouth, and either choke it or destroy its gills. Instead, however, of setting about its work in such a violent manner, the salmon moves through the water, and performs its duties quietly and unostentatiously; the fish sustaining no injury beyond the slight abrasions on the tail, the fins, and cheeks, necessarily produced by coming in frequent contact with the gravel.

M. Do all salmon and grilse come to the rivers for the purpose of spawning?

H. We see that salmon and grilse come to the rivers for the purpose of spawning, and as the laws of Nature are perfect, we must conclude that they all come for that purpose, as they are charged either with roe or milt. Some people assert, without having produced any facts to substantiate their conclusions, that salmon spawn in the sea. I should like to put a few cross-questions to any one maintaining this notion, and ask him—Was it at high-water mark, or at low-water mark, or during the spring-tides, or neap-tides, you saw the fish spawning in the sea? or did you have yourself let down in a patent diving-bell to quietly contemplate the mysteries of the deep *en philosophe*, with sixty fathoms of water overhead? I might, with equal assurance, assert that herrings and cod-fish spawn partly in the sea and partly in the rivers; but my assertion would make me appear ridiculous, because the fact that they did not do so is so *notoriously* known to be contrary to fact and Nature. So also does the same imputation apply to those who attempt to separate the nature and habits of salmon, and give them two instincts, to suit their own theories, and with an eye to their interests, no doubt.

APPENDIX. 177

M. Do grilse spawn by themselves, and in rivers, as salmon do?

H. I have already hinted at the difference of instinct between salmon and grilse, by making one a spring and the other a summer fish, although in their habits they are precisely the same, each coming to the rivers and ascending them as far as they can, and there depositing their spawn precisely as the salmon do, at the same time keeping distinct from them as a separate family. The only way to arrive at the truth is to watch the burns and discover the bed of one pair only where they would be easily captured, which would set the matter at rest. This, to my knowledge, has been frequently done, and uniformly resulted in the same fact—viz. either two salmon were found together, or two grilse, which is very different from the vague statements of those who profess to arrive at conclusions from seeing a number of fish spawning on fords in large rivers, or capturing one fish with the leister, the fellow escaping in the crowd of other fishes.

M. Why is it that people assert that salmon spawn with grilse or with trout, and that they do not make a fuss about the operations of sea fishes and land animals?

H. Therein consists the absurdity of theorising without consulting nature at all. If you look to the different tribes of animals, birds, and fishes, you will find that each family adheres strictly to its own members, and never intermixes with the tribe. For instance, a sparrowhawk keeps itself distinct from the gosshawk, the gosshawk from the harrier, the harrier from the gled, the gled from the osprey, and the osprey from the golden eagle. In like manner, the innumerable branches of the families of antelopes observe the laws of nature, keeping separate and distinct, and thereby perpetuating the different kinds without ever running into an heterogeneous amalgamation. The same law applies to fishes. Yet were all these varieties of the hawk first seen by a person ignorant of their nature and habits, he would very likely, as people do regarding salmon and its many varieties, pronounce the sparrowhawk a young eagle, a rook a young raven, or a grilse a young salmon.

M. Do you believe that all the grilse and salmon that come into a river spawn?

H. As a general law of nature, all animals are subservient to the instincts and functions placed in them; and if salmon were not disturbed in the rivers, either by floods or by man, they would all accomplish the object for which they came to the rivers; but they are so frequently interfered with and interrupted in the process of their spawning operations, that all those who do not get that process accomplished before the middle of December have their object frustrated, and the spawn becomes vapid; so that if the ova in the salmon, called "*baggits,*" caught in the Tweed in the month of February, were to be conveyed to an experimental pond, my belief is, that it would prove addled and of no avail, as it would be an anomaly in the laws of nature to suppose that salmon had the power of prolonging the time of gestation to an indefinite period.

M. When do the parent fish leave the river? or is it necessary for them to superintend the education of the young fry?

H. They quit the rivers by degrees, extending over all the spring months, nor do they evince any great solicitude for the fry; if they did, they would require to remain in the river sixteen or seventeen months: but such solicitude is not necessary, as their instincts lead the young smolts in their journey to their destination. A more convincing proof of the powerful action of instinct can in no instance be more apparent than in the cuckoo. It makes its appearance about the commencement of May; it has never yet been known to build a nest for itself; it deposits its egg in another bird's nest, and disappears before its progeny has quitted its foster-mother's guardianship. Yet a few weeks thereafter the young bird also mysteriously disappears, without any assistance or guide but the force of instinct; showing that the *same* instinct leads to the *same* result, though not simultaneously. I could state some interesting facts relative to cuckoos; but that would be entering into *details* which is not my object, either as regards the salmon or the illustrations brought forward, to elucidate the mystery that obscures the difference between salmon and grilse.

M. Then do you believe that cuckoos are migratory?

H. No; I do not believe that any vague or non-gregarious birds or fishes are migratory; but that the cuckoo, like the stone-chatter and water-wagtail, is of hybernating habits—which is not more wonderful in the works of creation than that the bat, humble-bee, and other animals, should exist in a torpid state all winter. If we have so much difficulty in arriving at the true history of animals living in our own element, it is not to be wondered at that theorists, in their attempts to discover the habits of creatures of another element, should reject the laws of nature, and propagate opinions opposed to them, in accordance with their own theories.

M. How long do the fry remain in the rivers after vivifying?

H. Mr Shaw has proved that they remain in the rivers about twelve months before they proceed to the sea in March, April, and May. During those twelve months their appearance does not indicate that they have lived in an uncongenial element; for when they are intercepted on their way to the sea, they look round, fat, and plump, yet they do not measure much more, on an average, than five inches in length.

M. Then you repudiate the idea of their returning that year?

H. Yes; on the grand principle of the annual migratory system; which seems to be uniformly admitted as regards herrings, that visit the Caithness coast once in the twelve months, swallows, the teal-duck, lapwing, &c.; that is to say, that at a regular stated period of the year these creatures are invariably expected, and that they never fail to appear at that time, unless their progress is intercepted. So I believe that the smolt of the salmon requires one year at least to perform its migrations, to the North Sea it is supposed, and at the expiry of that time it returns as a salmon; for it seems quite contrary, indeed, in direct opposition to, the law of migration, to suppose that they do not migrate at all, but only remain in the sea for a period of two months, at the expiry of which time they return to the rivers weighing three or five pounds. An authority on this subject says that salmon run to the sea and back again at pleasure, like shuttlecocks, when they find themselves growing either too fat or too thin. But before we can bring ourselves to accept such a theory, we must entirely give up the idea of salmon being a migratory fish, and indeed resign ourselves to the necessity of depriving it of instinct altogether. Yet were the supporters of these specious theories and quibbles deliberately to think the matter over, they would find that in bringing back the entire produce of a year's spawning, as well of salmon as of grilse, within the period of two months, they would inevitably deprive themselves of a crop of salmon for the ensuing *spring* fishery.

M. Then you maintain that, when the *fry of salmon* descends to the sea, it does not return to the rivers in the shape of a grilse, but remains in the sea until it is a salmon, and that the *produce of grilse* only return as grilses.

H. I do. Let theorists bring back the grilse two months after they quitted the rivers as smolts, *if* they *will*, for the sake of their own theories; but let them, for their interests, leave the fry of salmon in the sea until they become salmon, and supply their fishery with salmon next spring. To explain to you more clearly what I mean, let us suppose that, at the commencement of the world, when the produce of the first year's spawning returned in summer, two months after they had left the river, whence was the spring fishery of the ensuing year to be supplied? for even admitting that the kelts, or spawned fish, came back in spring—when most of them are still in the rivers as kelts—after a brief stay in the sea, they would form but a sorry fishery, as they are well known to be in a half-emaciated state, with jagged gills, and parasites adhering to them, evidently exhibiting every symptom of fish that have recently spawned, without flavour, and devoid of the perfect symmetry which characterises the clean salmon.

M. It is admitted that salmon are degenerating, and that they will soon become a fish of history, unless the legislature step in to protect them. What measures would you suggest as best calculated to restore the rivers to what they were in the olden times?

H. Individual interests and opinions are so conflicting that it will be difficult, even for the legislature, to enact laws sufficiently stringent to secure so desirable an object, *unless they found them upon the old Scotch statutes;* and by strictly adhering to them as their guide, they cannot err, as those statutes are founded upon knowledge of the nature and habits of the salmon; providing against unlawful modes of extermination, as well as sufficiently guaranteeing an ample period for spawning-time, and protecting the spawning fish from poachers. These statutes were framed at a time when Scotland had a Parliament of her own in Edinburgh, and when the Legislators, intelligent men, residing on their estates all the year, except when they were assembled, were unquestionably capable of framing Acts to harmonise with the nature and habits of the salmon, and the requirements of the public, without prejudice to their own interests, or the ample supply of fish. Very different men from many of the representatives who are now sent to St Stephen's, whose first and only acts were the payments of their election bills. I would, however, suggest that all sheep-farmers should be compelled to abstain from washing sheep in rivers, a practice most detrimental to fish; and that they should be obliged to make ponds at a considerable distance from the rivers to wash their sheep in, a necessary adjunct to the sheep-farmer that could be constructed at a trifling expense. And further, that all salmon-fishings, whether in the sea or in rivers, should be restricted to coble and net, as sanctioned by use and wont. Unless this mode of fishing for salmon be inflexibly enforced, the salmon-fishery of Scotland will inevitably dwindle away, as it has done in England.

M. I have been told that poachers are much more successful in angling for salmon than are sportsmen; how can you account for it?

H. Timidity is a ruling feature in all wild creatures; and as with deer, so with salmon. A deerstalker has to keep out of view of the deer, and guard against the influence of the wind, to insure success. In precisely the same way the angler must not only keep out of view of the salmon in approaching the river, but even keep his rod as much in the background as possible, and cast his line from a distance, letting the fly alight on the water like a snow-flake. If the angler will practise this precaution, and not wade into the water—salmon having a keen sense of taste or smell—it will be owing to the scarcity of fish if he fails. I always went about my business in this style. But in the present day, not only do gentlemen not observe this precaution, but they order stone erections to be thrown out into the rivers at stated casts, to bring them into direct view of the fish. I repeat again, that the great secret in successful angling is to stalk the fish—and down river.

THE END.

Narrative of the Earl of Elgin's Mission to China and Japan.

By LAURENCE OLIPHANT,
Private Secretary to Lord Elgin.

In Two Volumes Octavo, price £2, 2s.

Illustrated with numerous Engravings in Chromo-Lithography, Maps, and Engravings on Wood, from Original Drawings and Photographs.

OPINIONS OF THE PRESS.

Blackwood's Magazine.

"The charm of this book is its perpetual life."
"We are delighted, however, to leave these official details, and dwell on the liveliest features of the book. When the author is left to his own discretion, we scarcely can banish the idea that we are reading a novel of life and manners. And such life, and such manners! so perfectly different from our own, and so unmistakably true."

Edinburgh Review.

"It is long since any spectacle has been disclosed to the observer of politics and of manners so novel and so interesting as that which Mr Oliphant affords us of the internal condition of Japan; and we cannot lay down his Second Volume without in some degree sharing in the enthusiasm and astonishment the aspect of the Japanese empire appears to have excited in his own mind. . . . . The volumes in which Mr Oliphant has related these transactions will be read with the strongest interest now, and deserve to retain a permanent place in the literary and historical annals of our time."

Athenæum.

"The account of the mission to Japan is absorbingly interesting. Indeed, the entire work, apart from mere commonplaces which were unavoidable, is one that must attract every reader who cares to note, under the guidance of an accomplished traveller, the manners and customs of two Eastern Empires, not more unlike the rest of the world than they are contrasts one to another."

Economist.

"Lord Elgin's Mission has been given to the public by Lord Elgin's private secretary, and a better historiographer for such an occasion could scarcely have been found. Mr Oliphant is an experienced traveller and a practised writer; he knows what to report, and how to report it; he enters on expeditions with the true spirit of a hardy and adventurous explorer, and he handles his pen with spirit, taste, and reticence."

Morning Post.

"If Mr Oliphant's diplomatic talents are on a par with his gifts as historiographer, Lord Elgin may well be proud of his private secretary. His narrative is an exquisite and most valuable addition to English literature. It is illustrated, and even printed, in a style of rare excellence. It is written with a masterly ease and command of the subject, with a perfect sense of what it is superfluous or inexpedient to say, and in a style which is rather vivid than picturesque."

The Press.

"That he has done his work well, is no more than the world had a right to expect from his previous publications; but the highest anticipations of his success are likely to fall short of the reality. In his former writings Mr Oliphant gave abundant evidence of manly enterprise, a genial temperament, and keen perceptions; but in the present work we are chiefly struck with the broad statesmanlike views he enunciates, the severe discrimination he evinces in preferring the useful to the entertaining, and his graphic power of description."

WILLIAM BLACKWOOD & SONS, EDINBURGH AND LONDON.

MESSRS BLACKWOOD & SONS'
PUBLICATIONS.

Complete Library Edition of Sir Edward
Bulwer Lytton's Novels.

In Volumes of a convenient and handsome form. Printed from a large readable type. Published monthly, price 5s. per Volume. Vols. I. to V. are published.

"It is of the handiest of sizes; the paper is good; and the type, which seems to be new, is very clear and beautiful. There are no pictures. The whole charm of the presentment of the volume consists in its handiness, and the tempting clearness and beauty of the type, which almost converts into a pleasure the mere act of following the printer's lines, and leaves the author's mind free to exert its unobstructed force upon the reader."—*Examiner.*

"Nothing could be better as to size, type, paper, and general getting up. The Bulwer Novels will range on the same shelf with the Scott Novels; and appearing, as these two series will do, together, and in a mode tempting readers, old and young, to go through them once again for pleasure and profit, will inevitably lead to comparison of the genius, the invention, the worldly knowledge, and artistic skill of the great Scottish and English writers."—*Athenæum.*

New General Atlas.
Keith Johnston's Royal Atlas of Modern Geography.

Part V., now published, contains—

    AUSTRIAN EMPIRE, Western Sheet, comprising Austria Proper, the Tyrol, Bohemia, Venetia, &c.
    AUSTRIAN EMPIRE, Eastern Sheet—Hungary, Galicia, Transylvania, the Servian Woiwodschafts, and the Banat of Temes, Slavonia, and the Military Frontier.
    NEW SOUTH WALES, SOUTH AUSTRALIA, & VICTORIA.
    OCEANIA, WESTERN AUSTRALIA, TASMANIA, & NEW ZEALAND.
    WEST INDIA ISLANDS & CENTRAL AMERICA.

This Atlas will be completed in Ten Parts, price 10s. 6d. each, and will form a handsome portable Volume, size 20×13½ inches, consisting of a series of 48 original and authentic Maps, constructed by ALEX. KEITH JOHNSTON, F.R.G.S., Author of the "Physical Atlas," &c., and beautifully engraved and coloured in the finest style by W. & A. K. JOHNSTON, with a Special Index to each Map.

A Cruise in Japanese Waters.
By Captain SHERARD OSBORN, C.B.,
Author of "Leaves from an Arctic Journal," "Quedah," &c.

A New Edition. Crown Octavo, price 5s.

"The fascination of this strange country was undoubtedly great, for it is transferred to every page of Captain Osborn's narrative."—*The Times.*

"One of the most charming little books that for many a day we have had the good fortune to peruse."—*Literary Gazette.*

"One lays down the book with an irresistible desire to pack up all one has and start at once for Japan."—*Evening Herald.*

"In reading many pages of this book we almost feel that the action of the events is proceeding before us. . . . . There is not a dull or uninteresting line in the book."—*Morning Herald.*

The Eighteen Christian Centuries.

By the Rev. JAMES WHITE.

Third Edition, with Analytical Table of Contents, and a Copious Index. Post Octavo, price 7s. 6d.

"He goes to work upon the only true principle, and produces a picture that at once satisfies truth, arrests the memory, and fills the imagination. When they (Index and Analytical Contents) are supplied, it will be difficult to lay hands on any book of the kind more useful and more entertaining."—*Times*, Review of first edition.

"At once the most picturesque and the most informing volume on Modern History to which the general reader could be referred."—*Nonconformist*.

"His faculty for distinguishing the wheat from the chaff, and of rejecting the useless rubbish, while leaving no stray grain unsifted, makes the 'Eighteen Christian Centuries' an invaluable manual alike to the old and young reader."—*Globe*.

"Mr White comes to the assistance of those who would know something of the history of the Eighteen Christian Centuries; and those who want to know still more than he gives them, will find that he has perfected a plan which catches the attention, and fixes the distinctive feature of each century in the memory."—*Wesleyan Times*.

History of France,

FROM THE EARLIEST PERIOD TO THE YEAR 1848.

By the Rev. JAMES WHITE,
Author of the "Eighteen Christian Centuries."

Post Octavo, price 9s.

"Mr White's 'History of France,' in a single volume of some 600 pages, contains every leading incident worth the telling, and abounds in word-painting whereof a paragraph has often as much active life in it as one of those inch-square etchings of the great Callot, in which may be clearly seen whole armies contending in bloody arbitrament, and as many incidents of battle as may be gazed at in the miles of canvass in the military picture-galleries at Versailles."—*Athenæum*.

"An excellent and comprehensive compendium of French history, quite above the standard of a school-book, and particularly well adapted for the libraries of literary institutions."—*National Review*.

"We have in this volume the history of France told rapidly and distinctly by a narrator who has fancy and judgment to assist him in seizing rightly and presenting in the most effective manner both the main incidents of his tale and the main principles involved in them. Mr White is, in our time, the only writer of short histories, or summaries of history, that may be read for pleasure as well as instruction, that are not less true for being told in an effective way, and that give equal pleasure to the cultivated and to the uncultivated reader."—*Examiner*.

Leaders of the Reformation:

LUTHER, CALVIN, LATIMER, AND KNOX.

By the Rev. JOHN TULLOCH, D.D.,
Principal, and Primarius Professor of Theology, St Mary's College, St Andrews.

Crown Octavo, price 5s.

"We are not acquainted with any work in which so much solid information upon the leading aspects of the great Reformation is presented in so well-packed and pleasing a form."—*Witness*.

"The idea was excellent, and most ably has it been executed. Each Essay is a lesson in sound thinking as well as in good writing. The deliberate perusal of the volume will be an exercise for which all, whether young or old, will be the better. The book is erudite, and throughout marked by great independence of thought. We very highly prize the publication."—*British Standard*.

"We cannot but congratulate both Dr Tulloch and the university of which he is so prominent a member on this evidence of returning life in Presbyterian thought. It seems as though the chains of an outgrown Puritanism were at last falling from the limbs of Scotch theology. There is a width of sympathy and a power of writing in this little volume which fills us with great expectation. We trust that Dr Tulloch will consider it as being merely the basis of a more complete and erudite inquiry."—*Literary Gazette*.

"The style is admirable in force and in pathos, and the book one to be altogether recommended, both for the merits of those of whom it treats, and for that which the writer unconsciously reveals of his own character."—*Globe*.

Lives of the Queens of Scotland,
AND ENGLISH PRINCESSES CONNECTED WITH THE REGAL SUCCESSION.

By AGNES STRICKLAND.

With Portraits and Historical Vignettes. Complete in Eight Vols., price £4, 4s.

History of Europe,
FROM THE COMMENCEMENT OF THE FRENCH REVOLUTION TO THE BATTLE OF WATERLOO.

By Sir ARCHIBALD ALISON, Bart., D.C.L.

A New Edition of the Library Edition is in the Press.
Crown Octavo Edition, 20 vols., price £6.
People's Edition, 12 vols., double cols., £2, 8s.; and Index Vol., 3s.

The History of Europe,
FROM THE FALL OF NAPOLEON TO THE ACCESSION OF LOUIS NAPOLEON.

By Sir ARCHIBALD ALISON, Bart., D.C.L.

Complete in Nine Vols., price £6, 7s. 6d. Uniform with the Library Edition of the Author's "History of Europe, from the Commencement of the French Revolution."

Atlas to Alison's History of Europe;
Containing 109 Maps and Plans of Countries, Battles, Sieges, and Sea-Fights. Constructed by A. KEITH JOHNSTON, F.R.S.E. With Vocabulary of Military and Marine Terms.

Library Edition, £3, 3s.; People's Edition, £1, 11s. 6d.

History of Greece under Foreign Domination.
By GEORGE FINLAY, LL.D., Athens.

Five Volumes Octavo—viz.:

Greece under the Romans. B.C. 146 to A.D. 717. A Historical View of the condition of the Greek Nation from its Conquest by the Romans until the Extinction of the Roman Power in the East. Second Edition, 16s.

History of the Byzantine Empire. A.D. 716 to 1204; and of the Greek Empire of Nicæa and Constantinople, A.D. 1204 to 1453. Two Volumes, £1, 7s. 6d.

Mediæval Greece and Trebizond. The History of Greece, from its Conquest by the Crusaders to its Conquest by the Turks, A.D. 1204 to 1566; and History of the Empire of Trebizond, A.D. 1204 to 1461. Price 12s.

Greece under Othoman and Venetian Domination. A.D. 1453 to 1821. Price 10s. 6d.

"His book is worthy to take its place among the remarkable works on Greek history, which form one of the chief glories of English scholarship. The history of Greece is but half told without it."—*London Guardian.*

"His work is therefore learned and profound. It throws a flood of light upon an important though obscure portion of Grecian history. . . . In the essential requisites of fidelity, accuracy, and learning, Mr Finlay bears a favourable comparison with any historical writer of our day."—*North American Review.*

Works of Professor Wilson.
Edited by his SON-IN-LAW, PROFESSOR FERRIER.

In Twelve Vols. Crown Octavo, price £3, 12s.

The following are sold separately:—

NOCTES AMBROSIANÆ. Four Vols. 24s.
ESSAYS, CRITICAL AND IMAGINATIVE. Four Vols. 24s.
RECREATIONS OF CHRISTOPHER NORTH. Two Vols. 12s.
TALES. One Vol. 6s.
POEMS. One Vol. 6s.

Works of Samuel Warren, D.C.L.
Uniform Edition, Five Vols., price 24s.

The following are sold separately:—

DIARY OF A PHYSICIAN. 5s. 6d.
TEN THOUSAND A YEAR. Two Vols. 9s.
NOW AND THEN. 2s. 6d.
MISCELLANIES. 5s.

Works of Thomas M'Crie, D.D.
Edited by his SON, PROFESSOR M'CRIE.

Uniform Edition, in Four Vols., Crown Octavo, price 24s.

The following are sold separately, viz.—

LIFE OF JOHN KNOX. 6s.
LIFE OF ANDREW MELVILLE. 6s.
HISTORY OF THE REFORMATION IN ITALY. 4s.
HISTORY OF THE REFORMATION IN SPAIN. 3s. 6d.
REVIEW OF "TALES OF MY LANDLORD," AND SERMONS. 6s.

Curran and his Contemporaries.
By CHARLES PHILLIPS, Esq., A.B.

A New Edition. Crown Octavo, price 7s. 6d.

"Certainly one of the most extraordinary pieces of biography ever produced. . . . No library should be without it."—*Lord Brougham.*
"Never, perhaps, was there a more curious collection of portraits crowded before into the same canvass."—*Times.*

Life of John, Duke of Marlborough,
WITH SOME ACCOUNT OF HIS CONTEMPORARIES.

By Sir ARCHIBALD ALISON, Bart., D.C.L.

Third Edition, Two Vols. Octavo, Portrait and Maps, 30s.

Poems and Ballads of Goethe.

Translated by PROFESSOR AYTOUN and THEODORE MARTIN.

Second Edition, price 6s.

"There is no doubt that these are the best translations of Goethe's marvellously-cut gems which have yet been published."—*The Times.*

Tales from "Blackwood."

Publishing in Monthly Numbers, price 6d., and in Volumes Quarterly, price 1s. 6d., bound in cloth.

The Volumes published contain—

VOL. I. The Glenmutchkin Railway.—Vanderdecken's Message Home.—The Floating Beacon—Colonna the Painter.—Napoleon.—A Legend of Gibraltar.—The Iron Shroud.

VOL. II. Lazaro's Legacy.—A Story without a Tail.—Faustus and Queen Elizabeth.—How I became a Yeoman.—Devereux Hall.—The Metempsychosis.—College Theatricals.

VOL. III. A Reading Party in the Long Vacation.—Father Tom and the Pope.—La Petite Madelaine.—Bob Burke's Duel with Ensign Brady.—The Headsman: A Tale of Doom.—The Wearyful Woman.

VOL. IV. How I stood for the Dreepdaily Burghs.—First and Last.—The Duke's Dilemma: A Chronicle of Niesenstein.—The Old Gentleman's Teetotum.—"Woe to us when we lose the Watery Wall."—My College Friends: Charles Russell, the Gentleman Commoner.—The Magic Lay of the One-Horse Chay.

VOL. V. Adventures in Texas.—How we got Possession of the Tuileries.—Captain Paton's Lament.—The Village Doctor.—A Singular Letter from Southern Africa.

VOL. VI. My Friend the Dutchman.—My College Friends—No. II.: Horace Leicester.—The Emerald Studs.—My College Friends—No. III.: Mr W. Wellington Hurst.—Christine: A Dutch Story.—The Man in the Bell.

VOL. VII. My English Acquaintance.—The Murderer's Last Night.—Narration of Certain Uncommon Things that did formerly happen to Me, Herbert Willis, B.D.—The Wags.—The Wet Wooing: A Narrative of '98.—Ben-na-Groich.

VOL. VIII. The Surveyor's Tale. By Professor Aytoun.—The Forrest-Race Romance.—Di Vasari: A Tale of Florence.—Sigismund Fatello.—The Boxes.

What will he do with it?

By PISISTRATUS CAXTON.

Second Edition. Four Vols. Post Octavo, price £2, 2s.

Adam Bede.

By GEORGE ELIOT.

Seventh Edition. Two Vols., Foolscap Octavo, price 12s.

Scenes of Clerical Life.

THE SAD FORTUNES OF AMOS BARTON—MR GILFIL'S LOVE STORY—JANET'S REPENTANCE.

By GEORGE ELIOT.

Second Edition. Two Vols., Foolscap Octavo, price 12s.

Lady Lee's Widowhood.

By LIEUT.-COLONEL E. B. HAMLEY.

With Engravings. Third Edition. Crown Octavo, price 6s.

Diversities of Faults in Christian Believers

By the Very Rev. E. B. RAMSAY, M.A., F.R.S.E.,
Dean of the Diocese of Edinburgh.

In Foolscap Octavo, price 4s. 6d.

Diversities of Christian Character.

Illustrated in the Lives of the Four great Apostles.

By the same Author.

Uniform with the above, price 4s. 6d.

Religion in Common Life:

A Sermon preached in Crathie Church, October 14, 1855, before Her Majesty the Queen and Prince Albert. Published by Her Majesty's Command.

By the Rev. JOHN CAIRD, D.D.

Bound in cloth, 8d. Cheap Edition, 3d.

Sermons.

By the Rev. JOHN CAIRD, D.D.,
Minister of West Park Church, Glasgow.

In Post Octavo, price 7s. 6d.

Prayers for Social and Family Worship.

Prepared by a Committee of the General Assembly of the Church of Scotland, and specially designed for the use of Soldiers, Sailors, Colonists, Sojourners in India, and other Persons, at Home or Abroad, who are deprived of the Ordinary Services of a Christian Ministry. Published by Authority of the Committee.

In Crown Octavo, bound in cloth, price 4s.

Prayers for Social and Family Worship.

Being a Cheap Edition of the above.

Price 1s. 6d.

Theism:

THE WITNESS OF REASON AND NATURE TO AN ALL-WISE AND BENE-FICENT CREATOR.—(BURNETT PRIZE TREATISE.)

By the Rev. J. TULLOCH, D.D.,
Principal, and Primarius Professor of Theology, St Mary's College, St Andrews.

Crown Octavo, 10s. 6d.

The Sketcher.

By the Rev. JOHN EAGLES, A.M., Oxon.

Originally published in *Blackwood's Magazine.*

In Post Octavo, price 10s. 6d.

"There is an earnest and vigorous thought about them, a genial and healthy tone of feeling, and a flowing and frequently eloquent style of language, that make this book one of the most pleasant companions that you can take with you, if you are bound for the woodland or pastoral scenery of rural England, especially if you go to study the picturesque, whether as an observer or as an artist."

Essays.

By the Rev. JOHN EAGLES, A.M., Oxon.

Originally published in *Blackwood's Magazine.*

Post Octavo, 10s. 6d.

Contents—

Church Music, and other Parochials—Medical Attendance, and other Parochials—A few Hours at Hampton Court—Grandfathers and Grandchildren—Sitting for a Portrait—Are there not great Boasters among us?—Temperance and Teetotal Societies—Thackeray's Lectures: Swift—The Crystal Palace—Civilisation: the Census—The Beggar's Legacy.

Thorndale: or, the Conflict of Opinions.

By WILLIAM SMITH,

Author of "A Discourse on Ethics," &c.

A New Edition. Crown Octavo, price 10s. 6d.

"More literary gems could be picked from this than almost any recent volume we know. It is a repository of select thoughts — the fruit of much reflection, much reading, and many years."—*Scotsman.*

"It is long since we have met with a more remarkable or worthy book. Mr Smith is always thoughtful and suggestive. He has been entirely successful in carrying out his wish to produce a volume, in reading which, a thoughtful man will often pause with his finger between the leaves, and muse upon what he has read. We judge that the book must have been written slowly, and at intervals, from its affluence of beautiful thought. No mind could have turned off such material with the equable flow of a stream. We know few works in which there may be found so many fine thoughts, light-bringing illustrations, and happy turns of expression, to invite the reader's pencil."—*Fraser's Magazine.*

Lectures on Metaphysics.

By Sir WILLIAM HAMILTON, Bart.

Edited by the Rev. H. L. MANSEL, B.D., and JOHN VEITCH, A.M.

In Two Vols., Octavo, price 24s.

Institutes of Metaphysic:

THE THEORY OF KNOWING AND BEING.

By JAMES F. FERRIER, A.B., Oxon.,

Professor of Moral Philosophy and Political Economy, St Andrews.

Second Edition. Crown Octavo, 10s. 6d.

Lays of the Scottish Cavaliers, and other Poems.

By W. EDMONDSTOUNE AYTOUN, D.C.L.,
Professor of Rhetoric and Belles-Lettres in the University of Edinburgh.

Twelfth Edition, price 7s. 6d.

"Mr Aytoun's *Lays* are truly beautiful, and are perfect poems of their class, pregnant with fire, with patriotic ardour, with loyal zeal, with exquisite pathos, with noble passion. Who can hear the opening lines descriptive of Edinburgh after the great battle of Flodden, and not feel that the minstrel's soul has caught the genuine inspiration?"—*Morning Post.*

Bothwell: A Dramatic Poem.

By the same Author.

Third Edition, price 7s. 6d.

The Ballads of Scotland.

Edited by Professor AYTOUN.

Second Edition. Two Volumes, price 12s.

"No country can boast of a richer collection of Ballads than Scotland, and no Editor for these Ballads could be found more accomplished than Professor Aytoun. He has sent forth two beautiful volumes which range with *Percy's Reliques*—which, for completeness and accuracy, leave little to be desired—which must henceforth be considered as the standard edition of the Scottish Ballads, and which we commend as a model to any among ourselves who may think of doing like service to the English Ballads."—*The Times.*

Firmilian; Or, the Student of Badajoz:

A SPASMODIC TRAGEDY.

Price 6s.

"Without doubt, whether we regard it as a satire or as a complete drama, *Firmilian* is one of the most finished poems of the day. Unity is preserved, and the intensity of the 'spasmodic' energy thrown into the narrative carries the reader through every page, while the graces of poetic fancy, and the touches of deep thought scattered throughout, challenge comparison with selections from the most modern poems."—*Liverpool Albion.*

The Book of Ballads.

Edited by BON GAULTIER.

Fifth Edition, with numerous Illustrations by DOYLE, LEECH, and CROWQUILL.

Gilt edges, price 8s. 6d.

The Russian Shores of the Black Sea
IN THE AUTUMN OF 1852, WITH A VOYAGE DOWN THE VOLGA, AND A TOUR THROUGH THE COUNTRY OF THE DON COSSACKS.
By LAURENCE OLIPHANT.
Octavo, with Engravings. Fourth Edition, 14s.

Minnesota and the Far West.
By LAURENCE OLIPHANT.
Octavo, with Illustrations, 12s. 6d.

Life in the Far West.
By G. F. RUXTON.
Foolscap, 4s.

Narrative of a Journey through Syria and Palestine.
By Lieutenant VAN DE VELDE.
Two Volumes, Octavo, with Maps, &c., 30s.

The Story of the Campaign of Sebastopol.
Written in the Camp, by Lieut.-Col. E. BRUCE HAMLEY.
Octavo, with Coloured Illustrations, 21s.

Three Years in California.
By J. D. BORTHWICK.
With Eight Illustrations by the Author. Octavo, 14s.

Salmon-Casts and Stray Shots:
BEING FLY-LEAVES FROM THE NOTE-BOOK OF JOHN COLQUHOUN, Author of the "Moor and the Loch," &c.
Second Edition, Foolscap, 5s.

The Chemistry of Common Life.

By PROFESSOR JOHNSTON.

A New Edition, Edited by G. H. LEWES.

Illustrated with numerous Engravings. In Two Vols. Foolscap, price 11s. 6d.

The Physiology of Common Life.

By GEORGE H. LEWES.

Illustrated with numerous Engravings. Vol. I., 6s.

Contents— Hunger and Thirst.—Food and Drink.—Digestion and Indigestion.—The Structure and Uses of the Blood.—The Circulation.—Respiration and Suffocation.—Why we are Warm, and how we keep so.—Feeling and Thinking.—The Mind and the Brain.—Our Senses and Sensations.—Sleep and Dreams.—The Qualities we Inherit from our Parents.—Life and Death.

The Physical Atlas of Natural Phenomena.

By ALEX. KEITH JOHNSTON, F.R.S.E., &c.,

Geographer to the Queen for Scotland.

A New and Enlarged Edition, consisting of 35 Folio Plates, 27 smaller ones, printed in Colours, with 135 pages of Letterpress, and Index.

Imperial Folio, half-bound morocco, £12, 12s.

Atlas of Astronomy.

A complete Series of Illustrations of the Heavenly Bodies, drawn with the greatest care from Original and Authentic Documents, and printed in Colours by Alex. Keith Johnston.

Edited by J. R. HIND.

Imperial Quarto, half-bound morocco, 21s.

A Geological Map of Europe.

By Sir R. I. MURCHISON, D.C.L., M.A., F.R.S., &c., and

JAMES NICOL, F.R.S.E., F.G.S.,

Professor of Natural History in the University of Aberdeen.

Constructed by ALEX. KEITH JOHNSTON.

On Four Sheets Imperial, beautifully printed in Colours. Size, 4 feet 2 by 3 feet 5 inches. Price in Sheets, £3, 3s.; in a Cloth Case, Quarto, £3, 10s.

The Book of the Farm.

By Henry Stephens, F.R.S.E.

A New Edition. In Two Volumes, large Octavo, with upwards of 600 Engravings, price £3, half-bound.

"The best practical book I have ever met with."—*Professor Johnston.*
"One of the completest works on agriculture of which our literature can boast."—*Agricultural Gazette.*

Book of Farm Implements and Machines.

By James Slight and R. Scott Burn.
Edited by Henry Stephens, F.R.S.E.

Illustrated with 876 Engravings. One large Volume, uniform with the "Book of the Farm," price £2, 2s.

"The author has omitted, most judiciously, those machines not now used, and he has confined himself to those in actual operation, thereby rendering a great service to the agricultural mind, which is liable to confusion in cases of much complication. Some of the machines described are commended, and deserve the commendation; others, on the contrary, are condemned, and it would seem with equal justice: but the character of all is stated distinctly. . . . . Full, complete, and perfect in all its parts; honestly compiled, and skilfully illustrated with numerous and valuable engravings and diagrams, it is not saying too much to state that there is no parallel to this important work in any country of Europe, and that its value to the agriculturist is almost incalculable."—*Observer.*

The Book of the Garden.

By Charles M'Intosh.

In Two large Volumes, Royal Octavo, published separately.

Vol. I.—On the Formation of Gardens—Construction, Heating, and Ventilation of Fruit and Plant-Houses, Pits, Frames, and other Garden Structures, with Practical Details, illustrated by 1073 Engravings, pp. 776. Price £2, 10s.

Vol. II.—PRACTICAL GARDENING contains: Directions for the Culture of the Kitchen Garden, the Hardy Fruit Garden, the Forcing Garden, and Flower Garden, including Fruit and Plant Houses, with Select Lists of Vegetables, Fruits, and Plants. Pp. 868, with 279 Engravings. Price £1, 17s. 6d.

The Year-Book of Agricultural Facts.

Edited by R. Scott Burn.

In Foolscap Octavo, price 5s.

A Handy Book on Property Law.

By Lord St Leonards.

A New Edition, enlarged, with Index, Crown Octavo, price 3s. 6d.

"Less than 200 pages serve to arm us with the ordinary precautions to which we should attend in selling, buying, mortgaging, leasing, settling, and devising estates. We are informed of our relations to our property, to our wives and children, and of our liabilities as trustees or executors, in a little book for the million, a book which the author tenders to the *profanum vulgus* as even capable of 'beguiling a few hours in a railway carriage.'"—*The Times.*

Works of Professor J. F. W. Johnston.

A Catechism of Agricultural Chemistry and Geology.
Fifty-Second Edition, with numerous Engravings on Wood, price 1s.

Elements of Agricultural Chemistry and Geology.
Seventh Edition, Foolscap, price 6s. 6d.

Instructions for the Analysis of Soils, Minerals, Manures, &c.
Fourth Edition, Foolscap, price 3s.

On the Use of Lime in Agriculture.
Foolscap, price 6s.

Experimental Agriculture:
BEING THE RESULTS OF PAST AND SUGGESTIONS FOR FUTURE EXPERIMENTS IN SCIENTIFIC AND PRACTICAL AGRICULTURE.
Octavo, price 8s.

Notes on North America—
AGRICULTURAL, ECONOMICAL, AND SOCIAL.
Two volumes, Post Octavo, price 21s.

Rural Economy of England, Scotland, and Ireland.
By LEONCE DE LAVERGNE.
Translated from the French. With Notes by a Scottish Farmer.
Octavo, price 12s.

The Architecture of the Farm:
A SERIES OF DESIGNS FOR FARM HOUSES, FARM STEADINGS, FACTORS' HOUSES, AND COTTAGES.
By JOHN STARFORTH, Architect.
Sixty-two Engravings. Medium Quarto, price £2, 2s.

Catechism of Practical Agriculture.
By HENRY STEPHENS, F.R.S.E., Author of the "Book of the Farm."
With numerous Engravings on Wood, price 1s.

The Yester Deep-Land Culture:
Being a detailed Account of the method of Cultivation which has been successfully practised for several years by the Marquess of Tweeddale at Yester.
By HENRY STEPHENS, F.R.S.E., Author of the "Book of the Farm."
Foolscap, price 4s. 6d.

Stable Economy:
A TREATISE ON THE MANAGEMENT OF HORSES.
By JOHN STEWART, V.S.
Sixth Edition, Foolscap, price 6s. 6d.

The Geology of Pennsylvania.

A Government Survey; with a General View of the GEOLOGY OF THE UNITED STATES, Essays on the Coal-Formation and its Fossils, and a Description of the Coal-Fields of North America and Great Britain.

By Professor HENRY DARWIN ROGERS, F.R.S., F.G.S., Professor of Natural History in the University of Glasgow.

With Seven large Maps, and numerous Illustrations engraved on Copper and on Wood. In Three Volumes, Royal Quarto, £8, 8s.

Introductory Text-Book of Geology.
By DAVID PAGE, F.G.S.

Third Edition, with Engravings. In Crown Octavo, price 1s. 6d.

"It has not been often our good fortune to examine a text-book on science of which we could express an opinion so entirely favourable as we are enabled to do of Mr Page's little work."—*Athenæum.*

Advanced Text-Book of Geology.
DESCRIPTIVE AND INDUSTRIAL.

By DAVID PAGE, F.G.S.

Second Edition, enlarged, with numerous Engravings, 6s.

"An admirable book on Geology. It is from no invidious desire to underrate other works—it is the simple expression of justice, which causes us to assign to Mr Page's *Advanced Text-Book* the very first place among geological works addressed to students, at least among those which have come before us. We have read every word of it, with care and with delight, never hesitating as to its meaning, never detecting the omission of anything needful in a popular and succinct exposition of a rich and varied subject."—*Leader.*

"It is therefore with unfeigned pleasure that we record our appreciation of his *Advanced Text-Book of Geology.* We have carefully read this truly satisfactory book, and do not hesitate to say that it is an excellent compendium of the great facts of Geology, and written in a truthful and philosophic spirit."—*Edinburgh Philosophical Journal.*

"We know of no introduction containing a larger amount of information in the same space, and which we could more cordially recommend to the geological student."—*Athenæum.*

Handbook of Geological Terms and Geology.

By DAVID PAGE, F.G.S.

In Crown Octavo, price 6s.

"'To the student, miner, engineer, architect, agriculturist, and others, who may have occasion to deal with geological facts, and yet who might not be inclined to turn up half a dozen volumes, or go through a course of geological readings for an explanation of the term in question,' Mr Page has carried out his object with the most complete success. His book amply fulfils the promise contained in its title, constituting a handbook not only of geological terms but of the science of geology. It will not only be absolutely indispensable to the student, but will be invaluable as a complete and handy book of reference even to the advanced geologist."—*Literary Gazette.*

"There is no more earnest living practical worker in geology than Mr David Page. To his excellent *Introductory Text-Book of Geology* and his *Advanced Text-Book of Geology, Descriptive and Industrial,* he has now added an admirable system of geological terms, with ample and clearly-written explanatory notices, which as all geological observers, whether they are able professors and distinguished lecturers, or mere inquirers upon the threshold of the science, must find to be of the highest value."—*Practical Mechanics' Journal.*

"But Mr Page's work is very much more than simply a translation of the language of Geology into plain English; it is a Dictionary, in which not only the meaning of the words is given, but also a clear and concise account of all that is most remarkable and worth knowing in the objects which the words are designed to express. In doing this he has chiefly kept in view the requirements of the general reader, but at the same time adding such details as will render the volume an acceptable Handbook to the student and professed geologist."—*The Press.*

IN THE PRESS.

I.
Complete in Two Volumes,

PHYSIOLOGY OF COMMON LIFE.
By GEORGE HENRY LEWES,
Author of "Sea-Side Studies."

Illustrated with numerous Engravings; and a copious INDEX.

II.
A CHEAP EDITION OF

SEA-SIDE STUDIES.
By GEORGE HENRY LEWES,
Author of "Physiology of Common Life," &c.

III.

LECTURES ON THE HISTORY OF THE CHURCH OF SCOTLAND.
By THE LATE REV. JOHN LEE, D.D., LL.D.,
Principal of the University of Edinburgh.

In Two Volumes, Octavo.

IV.

THE BOOK OF FARM BUILDINGS:
THEIR ARRANGEMENT AND CONSTRUCTION.

By HENRY STEPHENS, F.R.S.E., AND R. SCOTT BURN.

In large Octavo, with numerous Engravings.

V.
A Third Edition, enlarged, of

THE FORESTER.
A PRACTICAL TREATISE ON THE FORMATION OF PLANTATIONS, THE PLANTING, REARING, AND MANAGEMENT OF FOREST TREES, ETC.

By JAMES BROWN,
Wood-Manager, Grantown, Strathspey.

IN THE PRESS.

VI.

A NEW NOVEL BY THE AUTHOR OF "ADAM BEDE."

THE MILL ON THE FLOSS.
By GEORGE ELIOT,
Author of "Scenes of Clerical Life," and "Adam Bede."
In Three Volumes.

VII.

ST STEPHENS:
A POEM.
ORIGINALLY PUBLISHED IN "BLACKWOOD'S MAGAZINE."

VIII.

CONQUEST AND COLONISATION IN NORTH AFRICA;
Being the substance of a Series of Letters from Algeria published in the *Times*, and now by permission collected.

With INTRODUCTION and SUPPLEMENT, containing the most recent French and other Information on Morocco.

By GEORGE WINGROVE COOKE,
Author of "China in 1857-1858."
With a Map.

IX.

FLEETS AND NAVIES.
By Captain CHARLES HAMLEY, R.M.
ORIGINALLY PUBLISHED IN "BLACKWOOD'S MAGAZINE."

X.

In Two Volumes, price 24s.,

LECTURES ON LOGIC.
By SIR WILLIAM HAMILTON, Bart.
Edited by the Rev. H. L. MANSEL, B.D., and JOHN VEITCH, A.M.

WILLIAM BLACKWOOD & SONS, EDINBURGH AND LONDON.

www.ingramcontent.com/pod-product-compliance
Lightning Source LLC
Chambersburg PA
CBHW020912230426
43666CB00008B/1420